BRINGING HEAVEN DOWN TO EARTH

365 MEDITATIONS OF THE REBBE

BRINGING
HEAVEN
DOWN
TO
EARTH

365 Meditations

from the teachings of the Rebbe
Menachem Mendel Schneerson

interpreted & compiled by Tzvi Freeman

4th printing
revised edition

copyright ©Tzvi Freeman, 1996, 1997
permissions & comments: tzviF@aol.com
website: www.theRebbe.com

order direct:
phone: 800 247-6553
email: order@bookmasters.com

ISBN 0-9682408-0-1

Class One Press
Vancouver, Canada/Berkeley, USA

Printed in the United States of America
by Thomson-Shore, Inc.

DEDICATION

*Many became leaders because
they brought others to believe in them.
The Rebbe was a great leader because
he believed so much in us. Putting this book
together is my way of trying not to let him down.*

DON'T READ THIS BOOK

As a searching adolescent immersed in the writings of Lao Tse, Richard Alpert, the Dali Lama and Alan Watts, I still felt a great sense of dissatisfaction—that something was missing from all this. G-d, a voice inside told me, has more to do with the material world in which I live. It was not until I came across the teachings of the Rebbe that I felt that sense of, "these are the words of my heart speaking from within".

I went to study in the yeshivas of the Rebbe for nine years, and continued learning for another ten while, thank G-d, raising a family and making a living.

On the 3rd of Tammuz, 5754 (June 12, 1994), the Rebbe passed on. I felt a need to gather the pieces of everything the Rebbe had given me, to package them in tight little parcels so they shouldn't be lost. Then I put them in this book. I looked at the book and found the Rebbe was still alive.

The Rebbe has been held prisoner too long in a little box of stereotype and preconception. People simply don't look in Brooklyn for modern day gurus—not at a rabbi in 18th century clothing. Perhaps had he hailed from the mountains of Tibet or taught psychoanalysis at Berkeley...

But he never even tried to make himself marketable. He didn't dress it, he didn't speak it and he didn't seem to want it. And so his light remained pure—but within.

This is how we'll liberate him, you and I:

Don't read this book. Live with it as I have. Make it a dialogue between the Rebbe and your life.

Take it little by little. When you need an answer, look here. When you need to come up for air, find it in the Rebbe's words. When life is getting tough and confusing, open up just anywhere—or choose a random number —and see what the Rebbe has to say.

If you find heaven, then do us all a favor and bring it down to earth.

Some of the lines in this book are direct quotations translated from the Yiddish. A few are words the Rebbe would commonly quote in the name of one of his predecessors. The bulk of this book, however, is composed of my own paraphrases of longer teachings.

CONTENTS

IN CONTEXT

IN CONTEXT

No one rises above the earth by tugging at his own hairs. A prisoner cannot free himself from his prison. He needs first to bond with one who is already free.

And so, at an early age, I was looking for someone who could guide me—a mentor, a guru. But who will be your guide when you beat your own path?

My path has always been like those of the deer in the forest—skipping over, squeezing and breaking through, steering far from the clear highways that everyone else travels.

On my fifteenth birthday I dropped out of high school. The year before I had been on the honor roll, and this year I was the grade ten president—but now I had no interest in following the established order.

When my parents made it clear that room and board were contingent upon my completing high school, I found a tutorial college that allowed me to take my exams that spring. And so, I found myself two years ahead of the game. Free—in my father's words—to associate with the fringe members of our society.

These were the early 70s in Vancouver—Canada's San Francisco. I gave classical guitar lessons and organized the "Anarchist Discussion Group" of the Vancouver Free University. I learned Tai Chi, Yoga, became a strict vegetarian, and attended countless "Encounter Groups". I hitch-hiked around Canada, the U.S., Israel, Europe and the U.K. I found souls travelling and dabbling on every kind of path I never had imagined.

I returned with a broader mind, but still a craving, empty soul. None of what I found was for me. When you search, it doesn't

matter where you look, the last thing you'll find is your own self.
I decided it was important to be able to do something well, and
for me that would be music. I approached a well-known composer
who lived in Vancouver for private lessons. She agreed, but after
a few sessions, commanded one of her graduate students to take
me by the hand and register me at the music college of the University
of British Columbia. This was not the place I wanted to be, but I
decided I would learn something. At the same time I began seriously
practicing meditation, teaching Yoga, and became fascinated
with Lao Tse.

Nevertheless, my soul's stomach was as empty as ever. Perhaps, I
wondered, what I need is to go off and hide in a Zen monastery
for a few years. The conflict of spirituality and sensuality, the
metaphysical and the material career was ripping me apart.
There was no real direction, only confusion. I remember praying
with all my heart—not for any answers, not for any
revelation—only that I should be able to talk heart to heart with
my G-d, because life in such a complicated, convoluted world
makes it very hard to talk sincerely with your G-d.

When a fish finds the ocean, it must dive in. When I first heard a
talk of chassidic mysticism, it didn't matter that I had no
comprehension of most of what was being said. Rain comes as a
stranger to a land parched for generations by drought, but the
earth remembers. What to my mind was foreign, to my guts was
home.

That first splash of native waters came from a travelling student of the Rebbe. I recall how he explained to me that our purpose was to perceive the G-dliness within every created thing. From between his words I perceived there was much more. At least a few thousand years of collective wisdom and beauty.

I wanted to know who taught this stuff. I wanted it explained to me. They told me there was a Rebbe in New York. "The Lubavitcher Rebbe".

"Rebbe" means a teacher. It is a term also used to refer to a master of the mystical path of Chassidic Judaism, as taught by the Baal Shem Tov.

"Lubavitch" is a town in Belorussia, a neighborhood in Brooklyn and an international association.

Lubavitch, the town, was the seat of a line of chassidic masters, rabbis who followed in the practical/mystical path of the Baal Shem Tov, as his teachings were elaborated by Rabbi Schneur Zalman of Liadi. At the outset of World War II, Lubavitch moved to Brooklyn.

"The Rebbe" is the title by which Rabbi Menachem Mendel Schneerson has come to be known by Jewry worldwide. He was the person most responsible for the miraculous revival of traditional Judaism after its near burial with the holocaust.

Menachem Mendel Schneerson was born in 1902 to Rebbetzin Chana Schneerson and the kabbalist and legalist, Rabbi Levi Yitzchaak Schneerson, chief rabbi of Dniprepetrovs'k in the Ukraine. He studied at home, because the teacher at the Jewish school complained he had nothing to teach him.

In his teen years, his father gave him permission to study science, mathematics and languages—but with the warning, "G-d forbid any of this should take away from your sixteen hours a day of Torah study."

Young Menachem passed the government matriculation exams six months later. He also acquired a working knowledge of English, Italian, French, Gruzian and Latin at this time.

From the years 1932 to 1940, the Rebbe studied the sciences and humanities at the University of Berlin and at the Sorbonne in Paris.

In 1941, he fled Nazi-occupied France for the U.S.A. For a short time he was employed as an engineer with the U.S. Navy. His work was labelled as "classified".

When the previous rebbe of Lubavitch passed away in 1950, the surviving remnants of Lubavitchers around the world turned immediately to his son-in-law, Rabbi Menachem Mendel Schneerson. Although he hid himself by dressing in modern clothes and avoiding any sort of prestige, they knew him as a great scholar and leader.

The chassidim begged that he take the leadership. He refused, repeatedly. He claimed he knew himself too well to imagine he might be fit for the job.

When a delegation of elder chassidim came with a petition accepting Rabbi Schneerson as their Rebbe,
he placed his head in his hands and began to cry. "Please, leave me alone," he begged. "This has nothing
to do with me."

It was only after one complete year of such episodes the Rebbe finally accepted the position. Even then it was with a condition: "I will help," the Rebbe announced, "But each of you must carry out your own mission. Don't expect to hang on to the fringes of my prayer shawl."

My first reaction was inspiration. I had to find out more about this man. After that, friends, relatives and acquaintances began to cool me off. They told me this was idol worship. They told me I was surrendering my power of thought and independence.

My intellect had to concur. Where was all my background in anarchist philosophy? After all, these were the reasons I had failed to follow any other guru or mentor more than a few steps. I did not want my mind taken away. I wanted my own path. I did not want to be swallowed alive by a larger ego.

That conflict continued for many years. There are some things you know inside, but the ego and all your rationalization refuses to allow that inner knowledge to take charge.

Nevertheless, today I find myself a chassid of the Rebbe and still my own self. The Rebbe just never matched the ego-consuming demagogue I had so much feared.

For one thing, the trappings were always conspicuously absent. No majestic, flowing robes. No magnificent estate. No private jet. A modest home in good taste and a bare bones office. Nothing on the outside to distinguish him from any of his chassidim.

He didn't need the big show. There was no ego involved. The Rebbe was a master of simplicity, at being nothing and just allowing the essential G-dliness of the soul to shine through. And so he was able to guide others without consuming them.

For many years, the Rebbe granted private audiences three nights a week. Aside from Lubavitcher chassidim, there was just about every kind of person you could imagine—Jewish activists, businessmen, scientists, politicians, journalists—awaiting their turn at two o' clock in the morning. The Rebbe talked warmly with each one, providing guidance and advice when solicited, blessings whether solicited or not.

The audiences began at eight in the evening and generally finished in the early morning. There were exceptions. One night it wasn't until 10:30 the next morning that the Rebbe finally broke for morning prayers. The following night was booked for more audiences. The Rebbe's personal secretary asked the Rebbe if he could put off that night and get some rest. But the Rebbe replied that he couldn't put off people who had been waiting so long.

The Rebbe kept a full day as usual. That night, the audiences went until 11 the next morning.

As for my rebellious spirit, in the Rebbe I found the ultimate rebel. I could even say, you don't submit to the Rebbe—you rebel with him. It's a long tradition of the rebbes of Lubavitch to defy the monster the world feigns to be, to follow an inner vision, rather than the superficial perception of the flesh eyes. It is no surprise that every one of the Rebbe's predecessors spent time in czarist or communist prison. The Rebbe himself was forced into hiding before leaving Russia.

The Rebbe was an orthodox rebel, a traditional radical. In the sixties, the rest of the Jewish Establishment looked on in disdain at what was happening to their youth and cried, "Student unrest! Hippies and Freaks! This is certainly a deranged and lost generation."

The Rebbe declared, "Finally the iceberg of America is beginning to melt! Finally, its young people realize they do not have to conform! They have smashed the idols of their parents—they need now only be led back to the living waters of their great-grandparents."

The Rebbe told his chassidim to go out and bring Jewish youth in touch with their roots. He was ridiculed for it for years. Only after the strategy began to work did those who had mocked him jump on the band wagon as well.

He was always a maverick, not consulting with others on his strategies and campaigns, often ridiculed for what they considered outrageous decisions.

"I am used to their tactics already," the Rebbe shot back.

"When I was a young boy, being the oldest son of the rabbi of a city in Russia, I was often taken for questioning by the authorities. They ridiculed me and showered me with abuse. I did not respond to any of their tactics. So too I will not respond to these."

The Rebbe took this radical attitude into his way of running things as well. Lubavitch became an organization where action came from the bottom up. Rarely, very rarely, did the Rebbe demand something specific be done. There were always suggestions. Chassidim were expected to take the initiative and do what they thought would work. Several times the Rebbe thwarted plans to create a rigid hierarchy of decision making within Lubavitch. Each person must find his mentor, and each mentor his mentor.

There were never any followers of the Rebbe—followers couldn't keep up. The Rebbe had only leaders. Those who rebelled with him.

Simchas Torah is a festive Jewish holiday. Every year at this time, the Rebbe's place of worship, 770 Eastern Parkway, Brooklyn, NY, packs in thousands of chassidim and all sorts of Jews celebrating with the Torah scrolls throughout the night, singing and dancing.

On Simchas Torah, 1977, amidst the festivities, the Rebbe turned pale. Suddenly, he turned from his place, walked through the entire hall, up the stairs, into his office and locked the door behind him. Only his wife was able to persuade him to unlock the door.

It became apparent that the Rebbe had suffered a heart attack. Typically, he had not wanted to disturb the festive mood.

The best doctors were immediately called. They had to come to the Rebbe, because the Rebbe refused to leave his office.

When the Rebbe asked what the people were doing in the synagogue downstairs, he was told they were crying and praying. He made a request: "Tell them the more they sing and dance, the better I will feel."

The chassidim danced and sang through the night like they never had before.

The Rebbe spent several weeks in his office under the doctors' care. It was noted that the healthiest activity for the Rebbe's heart was to study. The harshest activity was to read the letters that came to him. Many of the letters were from people in distress asking for blessing and advice. The Rebbe's heart would pulsate erratically in empathy for their sorrows.

When the doctors attempted to stop the delivery of letters to the Rebbe, the Rebbe intervened.

"You are trying to take away my livelihood," he protested.

It is all futile, I tell you. As long as you stand on the outside, how can I describe to you the relationship of a chassid with his Rebbe? There is a profound inner bond, dense with emotions all beyond words.

Look, here is my book. Yes, you'll say, the Rebbe's body is interred over three years now—but the bond is with his spirit and his spirit lives on even here in our world stronger than ever. By living with this book perhaps you could taste of that bond.

And then we may discuss what I have failed to put into words.

A well-known author came for a private audience with the Rebbe. After he left the Rebbe's office, he turned to the chassidim, and accused them, "You are thieves! You are stealing from the entire world! You have taken the Rebbe and made him exclusively your own, as though he were a Rebbe just for you Lubavitch Chassidim—"

"But the Rebbe is the Rebbe of the entire world!"

Let us liberate him, you and I.

—Tzvi Freeman, Tammuz 5757, Vancouver

FUSION

The teachings of the Rebbe are not just a collection of advice and nice thoughts—just as a year is more than the sum of 365 days. The teachings of the Rebbe make up one simple whole. All revolve around the same essential concept: The fusion of the loftiest spiritual heights with the most mundane physicality. In the Rebbe's words, "the highest with the lowest".

The concept is not only radical but powerful: It means I can be myself, living a "down to earth" existence, and yet fulfilling a transcendental goal. It means that there is nothing we are trying to escape—other than the notion that we must escape something. We don't run away from this world to join a higher one, instead we work to fuse the two. We aren't in the business of "making it to heaven"—we're busy bringing heaven down to earth.

1.

When it all began, Heaven was here on Earth.

The physical plane, more than any of the higher spiritual worlds, was the place where the Divine Presence yearned to be.

But Man, step by step, banished the Divine Presence from its home, with a tree of knowledge, with a man who murdered his brother, with all those things that human beings do...

Since Man chased it away, only Man can bring it back. And this began with Abraham, who proclaimed Oneness for all the world.

And it ends with us. Our generation will bring Heaven back down to Earth.

2.

Each generation has its role in history.

From all the generations before us we inherited a wealth of dreams: philosophy, truths, wisdom and purpose. We are tiny midgets standing on the shoulders of their ideas and their noble deeds.

Our generation's mandate—and destiny—is to make the dream real.

3.

One who has studied the Kaballa knows there are infinite worlds beyond ours and beyond the worlds of the angels, all full of divine light, beauty and oneness.

But know also that all this was brought into being with a single purpose: G-d desires to be at home within your mundane world.

4.

Animals do not gaze at the stars and angels are confined to the realm of the spirit, but Man is G-d's bridge between heaven and earth.

Our bodies are formed from the dust, our souls are of the essence of G-d. We alone can look at a physical world and see spiritual life and beauty. We who are beyond both heaven and earth, form and matter, spirit and body—we alone can fuse the two.

5.

Man sees a tree and the tree says, "I am here, I was here, and I am nothing more but a thing that is here."

And Man ponders and answers, "No! I give you a name! You are "tree"! You have beauty and you have a soul. You point upwards and you say, "There is something higher, there is the One who gives me life and gives me my very being."

And so Man goes on, until he has brought the whole of creation down on its knees.

Man alone can accomplish what the angels cannot. Man alone can discover the spiritual within the material.

6.

They have banished G-d into exile.

They have decreed He is too holy, too transcendent to belong in our world.

They have determined He does not belong within the ordinary, in the daily run of things.

And so they have driven Him out of His garden, to the realm of prayer and meditation, to the sanctuaries and the secluded places of hermits.

They have sentenced the Creator to exile and His creation they have locked in a dark, cold prison.

And He pleads, "Let me come back to my garden, to the place in which I found delight when it all began."

7.

There are people who do much good, but with pessimism—because to them the world is an inherently bad place.

They do good things, but without light and vitality. Who knows how long it can last?

We must know that this world is not a dark, sinister jungle, but a garden. And not just any garden, but G-d's own pleasure garden, full of beauty, wonderful fruits and fragrances, a place where G-d desires to be with all His essence.

It is only that we must break through the thorny husks, shells and peels to discover the fruit inside.

8.

The higher something is, the lower it falls. So too, the loftiest revelations are to be found in the lowest places.

Therefore, if you find yourself in a place seemingly devoid of anything spiritual—don't despair. The lower you are, the higher you can reach.

9.

The ultimate goal of the creation of all worlds lies in the lowest, most mundane physical realm. To elevate a structure, you cannot pull from the top—you must lift from the bottom.

10.

G-d is not just *big*—He is infinite. If He were only *big*, then those things that are small would be further from Him and those things that are big would be closer. But to the Infinite, big and small are irrelevant terms. He is everywhere and He is found wherever He wishes to be found.

11.

When I first arrived at Yeshiva, I threw myself entirely into the experience. Soon I realized I had lost my balance. It was at that time I heard these words of the Rebbe and they guided me:

The Talmud tells, "Four entered into the orchard (the mystical teachings). One died, one went mad and one became a heretic. Rabbi Akiva entered in peace and left in peace".

Why was Rabbi Akiva capable of leaving in peace? Because he entered in peace: He had made peace between his physical and spiritual worlds, between his body and his soul, and saw purpose in them both.

So when he entered the spiritual he had in mind his return to the physical. And when he re-entered the physical he brought with him of the spiritual.

12.

Every person is a microcosm of the entire Creation. When a person brings harmony between his G-dly soul and his material life, he brings harmony between the whole of heaven and earth.

13.

Rabbi Schneur Zalman of Liadi, the first rebbe of the Lubavitch dynasty, led the services for Yom Kippur, the holiest day of the year. He stood wrapped in his prayer shawl, profoundly entranced in the cleaving of the soul to its source. Every word of prayer he uttered was fire. His melody and fervor carried the entire community off to the highest and the deepest journey of the spirit.

And then he stopped. He turned, cast off his prayer shawl and left the synagogue. With a bewildered congregation chasing behind, he walked briskly to the outskirts of town, to a small dark house from where was heard the cry of a newborn infant. The rabbi entered the house, chopped some wood and lit a fire in the oven, boiled some soup and cared for the mother and child that lay helpless in bed.

Then he returned to the synagogue and to the ecstasy of his prayer.

...

(Note that the rabbi removed his prayer shawl. To help someone, you must leave your world of prayer and meditation and enter that person's world. You cannot help another from above, only from within.)

14.

In the ancient Book of Formation, it is written, "If your heart races, return to One."

There are times when you find yourself in a state of inspiration, uplifted from the banalities of everyday life. At this time you must "return to One"—to the oneness of heaven and earth: You must resolve how this heavenly state will affect your earthly life.

15.

First there was One. There was no peace, because there was nothing with which to make peace. There was only One.

Then there was Two. There was Plurality. From this point on, an infinite cacophony of conflict extended in all directions and forever.

And on the third day G-d created peace.

Peace is not homogeneity. Peace does not mean that everyone thinks the same way. Peace is when there is plurality that finds a higher Oneness.

16.

There are three ways to bring unity between two opposites:

The first is by introducing a power that transcends both of them and to which they both utterly surrender their entire being. They are then at peace with each other because they are both under the influence of the same force. But their *being* is not at peace—their *being* is simply ignored.

The second way is by finding a middle ground where the two beings meet. The two are at peace where they meet on that middle ground—but the rest of their territory remains apart and distant.

The third way is to reveal that the essence of every aspect of the two beings is one and the same. This is the way of Torah. Torah makes peace between the spiritual and the material by revealing that the true substance of all things is the Oneness of their Creator.

17.

In my first years studying in Lubavitch, I met other musicians who had also come to learn. We began to play together, eventually forming the first Chassidic Hard Rock Group, which we called, "The Baal Shem Tov Band". The formula was simple: We took traditional chassidic melodies and played them with a rock beat and rock harmonies at high distortion amplitudes. We had a good time. A reporter from the Village Voice even wrote that we were "electric".

Eventually, we adopted into our band a Moroccan drummer and vocalist who had starred in one of the top bands in France. He told us how he had first come to speak with the Rebbe, with beads and sequins and hair to his knees. He told the Rebbe he wanted to abandon his music and return to the religious life of his childhood home.

The Rebbe answered him:

"Everything has purpose. Whatever you have picked up on your journey, if it is not evil, you must find in it the Divine. On the contrary, you must use your rock music for good things, and that way you will sublimate the world of rock"

PURPOSE/ LIGHT

There is a recurring theme in the volumes of stories told of the Rebbe: The tale of the man who was in the right place at the right time.

You'll find it over and over. Either someone was embarking on a trip to some distant place, and the Rebbe gave him a book to take along, or asked him to do a certain thing there, or to meet a certain person. Or the Rebbe simply asked someone to go to a place, with little direction of what to do there.

And then, in these stories, it always works out that just at the right time the right person turns up in the right place and all the story unfolds.

It's all a matter of making connections: Every soul has certain sparks of light scattered throughout the world that relate to it in particular. The Rebbe sees the soul and senses, like a geiger counter, the sparks that await this soul. All that was needed is to bring the two within a reasonable proximity and the rest takes care of itself.

The stories are meant as a teaching as well. The Rebbe was revealing to us the wonder of our own lives, that there is purpose latent in whatever you are doing, wherever and whenever.

18.

The mandate of the whole of Creation is stated almost immediately: And G-d said, "It should become Light".

The purpose of Creation is that all the world—even the darkness—should become light.

19.

It all began with an infinite light that filled all and left no room for a world to be. Then that light was withheld so the world might be created in the resulting void.

Then the world was created, with the purpose of returning to that original state of light—yet to remain a world.

20.

All the world's problems stem from light being withheld.

Our job then, is to correct this. Wherever we find light, we must rip away its casings, exposing it to all, letting it shine forth to the darkest ends of the earth.

Especially the light you yourself hold.

21.

G-d did not give you light that you may hold it up in
the middle of the day. When you are given light it is in
order to *accomplish* something, to do something
difficult and novel. Go take your light and transform
the darkness that it may also shine!

22.

When you come to a place that seems outside of G-d's
realm, too coarse for light to enter, and you want to
run away. . .

Know that there is no place outside of G-d, and rejoice
in your task of uncovering Him there.

23.

Fighting evil is a very noble activity when it must be
done. But it is not our mission in life. Our job is to
bring in more light.

24.

At one time there were tzaddikim who would look into
the soul of a disciple, see the place where the G-dly
sparks were awaiting this soul and tell the disciple to
go to that place to liberate those sparks.

All that has changed is the perception of the disciples.
If you are where you are with the blessing of the
Rebbe, you are where you belong. And you are there
with a profound purpose.

25.

The teaching of the Baal Shem Tov: Not only is the movement of a leaf as it falls off a tree, the quivering of a blade of grass in the wind—each and every detail of existence directed, vivified and brought into being at every moment from above—but beyond that: Every nuance is an essential component of a grand and G-dly scheme, the gestalt of all those vital minutiae.

Meditate on this. And then think: How much more so the details of my daily life.

26.

For hundreds of years—perhaps since the beginning of Creation—a piece of the world has been waiting for your soul to purify and repair it.

And your soul, from the time it was first emanated and conceived, waited above to descend to this world and carry out that mission.

And your footsteps were guided to reach that place. And you are there now.

27.

The Baal Shem Tov taught that each of our lives is comprised of 42 journeys, corresponding to the 42 journeys of the Children of Israel in the wilderness.

Some of those journeys have pleasant names. Others don't sound so nice. But none are inherently bad. It is only that you may have to dig deeper and deeper to find the purpose and the good within them.

28.

In each journey of your life you must *be* where you are. You may only be passing through on your way to somewhere else seemingly more important —nevertheless, there is purpose in where you are right now.

29.

Purify time. Each day, find an act of kindness and beauty that belongs to that day alone.

30.

Every moment has two faces:

It is a moment defined by the past from which it extends and by the future to which it leads.

And it is a moment for itself, with its own meaning, purpose and life.

Don't kill a moment.

31.

People want to run away from where they are, to go to find their Jerusalem. Wherever you are, whatever you are doing there, make *that* a Jerusalem.

32.

When you run from the responsibility of one place to
be in another, two things are amiss: The place where
you are needed, and the place where you are and
shouldn't be.

33.

*To a young teacher who had recently accepted a post
teaching children in an isolated community, and
now wished to abandon his place to be closer to the
Rebbe:*

The Baal Shem Tov taught that a soul may descend
into this world for 70–80 years, just to do a favor for
another. You are there only a few months and have
performed so many favors for so many others—yet all
you can think of is abandoning it?!

34.

If you see what needs to be repaired and how to repair
it, then you have found a piece of the world that G-d
has left for you to complete. But if you only see what is
wrong and how ugly it is, then it is yourself that needs
repair.

35.

A certain chassid who had suffered a major financial loss stood before Rabbi Schneur Zalman of Liadi and lamented over his debts.

"All you are telling me," Rabbi Schneur Zalman replied, "is what *you* need. *Who needs you*, you don't say much about. Do what G-d expects from you, and He will provide what you want from Him."

36.

A chassid of the Rebbe once left a paper propped at the door of the Rebbe's office, expecting the Rebbe's secretary to notice it and take it in. The secretary failed to notice it, and instead the Rebbe himself stooped down to pick up the paper. The chassid apologized profusely for causing the Rebbe such trouble. The Rebbe replied,

"Isn't this my whole job in life—to pick up the things others have left fallen behind?"

Purpose/Light

NATURE
& THE
MIRACULOUS

There is a thread here, a chain of souls with a common mission, each one completing what the other left undone.

Seven generations back, 200 years ago, lived the first Schneerson, Rabbi Schneur Zalman of Liadi. Schneur Zalman was a great philosopher with the unique ability to draw into the words of intellect that which others could only feel deep in the soul. So he wrote a short book—a classic now known as "The Tanya"—in which he explained how there is nothing but G-d.

He explained that every detail of existence is constantly created at every moment, each detail by a particular force of G-d invested within it. He asserted that if the force of existence of any thing would be removed, that thing would cease to exist. As a matter of fact, he points out, that thing would never have existed—its past would also cease, since time, too, is a creation.

Which means that everything that happens comes from Above. Which means that G-d can be found anywhere, at any time, in any thing and by anybody. Which means that the greatest miracle is not to split the Red Sea or to stop the sun in its path, but the very fact that we all continue to exist. Because every moment we are all created anew, something from nothing.

All of which got him into a lot of trouble. Many people thought it was blasphemous to say that G-d should be found everywhere. He claimed these were things that Jews had always believed in their heart, but simply were unable to articulate. And he supported everything he said with Talmudic (as well as kabalistic) sources.

Eventually, even the students of opposing teachings accepted his views,, which swiftly became mainstream thought. The ideas found their way into secular thought as well. Today, nobody even realizes where the idea of constant creation came from.

So when the Rebbe expressed these same thoughts, and applied them to modern life, he came by them honestly. They were in his blood.

37.

Existence is the greatest of all miracles: At every moment, each thing comes again into being from absolute void. In truth, the essence of each thing is the Nothingness from whence it comes.

So what is so impossible about that which is truly nothing behaving as nothing? Why is it easier to accept the existence of the world than it is to accept the occurrence of miracles?

38.

We take the laws of nature too seriously. We think of the world as though it exists just as its Creator exists.

A miracle is a state of enlightenment that says, "Our reality is nothing but a glimmer of a Higher Reality. In that Higher Truth, there is no world. There is nothing else but Him."

39.

"World" in Hebrew is עולם "Olam". Olam means a place of concealment. The world appears as a place autonomous of its Creator—in other words, it appears to be a world—only by virtue of its concealment of the truth.

40.

To grasp at knowing how we are to our Creator:

Meditate upon the ray of light that pierces through a window on a sunny day—and imagine how that ray exists engulfed within its source, the sun. So too, are the cosmos a nothingness absorbed within their Source, the Infinite Light.

Imagine the entire universe as a stream of conscious thought, and imagine how a single thought exists in its place of birth, within the depths of a Supernal Subconscious, a place before words, before things, where there is only One.

We created beings cannot perceive the Source with our flesh eyes, and so we see a world. But to the Source there is no being, no entity, only the Infinite Light.

Yes, we are here. But in the Higher Reality, there is nothing else but Him.

41.

When a parent loves a child,

He stoops down to the child, with such love, he leaves his language to speak the language of the child, he leaves his place to play the games of the child, he leaves his entire world and all the maturity he has gained in thirty, forty years or more to become excited, sincerely excited, by those things that excite the child, to react as the child reacts, to *live* with the child in the child's world with all his being...

But he is not a child. He is an adult, even as he plays with the child. Precisely *because* he is *truly* an adult, he can allow himself to be a child and remain an adult.

Our G-d feels our pain and our joy. He lives intimately with us in our world. Yet He is infinite, beyond all things—even as He lives in our world.

42.

The philosophers are only trying to be nice to G-d: They can't allow an Infinite Being to get His Complete Simple Unity messed up with a lowly, material, fragmented world.

And so they banish Him to the far, ethereal heavens, as removed as possible from our world. By their way of thinking, you can forget about miracles, prophecy or divine intervention in your life. G-d is just too far out there.

Those philosophers are fools. In their groping for the infinite, they have ended up with a G-d bound by the limitations of the human mind. In fact, the ultimate measure of the Infinite is that it can be found within the finite as well. G-d is *here now,* within every thing, and G-d is One.

43.

G-d is not Nature.

But Nature is G-dly.

When G-d makes a miracle, it is so that afterwards we may look at the natural order of things and say, "I recognize this. This is not what it appears to be. This, too, is a miracle."

44.

G-d is not something of a higher realm that you cannot reach Him. Nor is He made of stuff ethereal that you cannot touch Him. G-d is "That Which Is"—He is *here now*, everywhere, in every thing and in every realm—including that realm in which you live.

The only reason you do not perceive Him is because it is His desire that you search for Him.

45.

Life is a game of hide and seek. G-d hides, we seek.

...

Everywhere in the world, parents play peek-a-boo with their children. It is a major discovery of life, a cornerstone in human development: To realize that something is there even when you cannot see it, that the world is not defined by your subjective perception, that there is something that absolutely *is*—whether you know of it or not.

All our life, all of the world, is G-d playing with us that same game. He peeks with a miracle and then hides behind nature. Eventually, we look behind nature to find Him there.

46.

The miracle of Chanuka was that one flask of oil burned for eight days.

Some say the oil burned, but new oil miraculously appeared each day.

Some say the oil wasn't really burning, that the *flame* was miraculous.

The theories go on and on.

Why do we limit G-d with our logic? Say simply the flame was burning oil, but the oil was not burning!

...

Explain to us your G-d.

-Our G-d cannot be explained.

That which cannot be explained cannot exist.

-Existence cannot be explained.

G-d can do anything. He could even, as the saying goes, "fit an elephant through the eye of a needle."

So, how would He do it? Would He make the elephant smaller? Or would He expand the eye of the needle?

Neither. The elephant would remain big, the eye of the needle small. And He would fit the elephant through the eye of the needle.

Illogical? True. But logic is just another of His creations. He who created logic is permitted to disregard it.

...

When the world was made and done, G-d was left with two lights: A light of boundless energy that encompasses all things and gives them being, but transcends them, and a penetrating light that vitalizes all things but is limited and darkened by them.

The first light is a pure expression of "there is none else but He", so from it extend miracles, acts that deny the world any significance.

The second light is an expression of His desire there be a world, so from it extends the natural order of things, a world of elements behaving as though they are directed by their own properties.

But G-d did not want a world where there are two gods—one of Nature and one of the supernatural. So He made the two lights to play in harmony, to reveal that they both shine from one Source.

How does He do it? Does He blunt the miracles so they could fit into the natural order? Or does He change the nature of things to compromise with the miracles?

Neither. The properties of each thing remain the same, the natural order runs according to its own laws, and miracles of the highest order occur. The elephant in the eye of the needle, the infinite within the finite.

Impossible? Plant a seed and watch it grow. And greater by order of magnitude: Plant good deeds and watch with wonder the miracles that ensue.

47.

To see water turn to blood, to watch as an entire sea
splits and stands as two walls, to be there when Joshua
made the sun stand still, the laws of nature entirely
abrogated...

Was to perceive an infinite force that leaves no room
for our finite universe.

To see G-d work miracles through nature in your
everyday life, on the other hand, is to see an infinite
force fitting within a finite place. Which means that He
is truly beyond both finite and infinite.

48.

There are two types of miracles: Those beyond nature
and those enclothed within it. The water of the Nile
turning into blood was beyond nature. The victory of
the Maccabees over the Greek army was enclothed
within nature—they had to fight to win.

Both types of miracles are necessary.

If we would only see miracles *beyond* nature, we
would know that G-d can do whatever He likes
—but we might think He must break the rules to do
so. We would know a G-d who is beyond nature, but
not within it.

If we would see only miracles that are *enclothed within*
nature, we would know that G-d is the Master of all
that happens within nature. But we might think He is
limited within it.

Now we know that G-d is at once both beyond and
within. In truth, there is nothing else but Him.

49.

There are open miracles that break the laws of nature as though they were meaningless—miracles any fool can perceive.

Then there are miracles that take some thought to realize, that, yes, something out of the ordinary occurred here.

And then there are miracles so great, so wondrous, that no one but G-d Himself is cognizant of them. They are the miracles that occur continuously, at every moment.

50.

The world is not predictable. Determinism is a leftover artifact of the nineteenth century. All we can say is that there are some loose rules by which G-d generally plays.

51.

The fall of the communist dictatorships of the Eastern
Bloc was a kind of miracle that has no historical
precedent. Never before were so many people affected
by such radical change with so little violence.

The miracles of the Gulf War were open miracles. The
same skud missiles that took countless lives in Iran
were impotent when they fell in the Holy Land. The
soldiers and officers of the Allied Forces saw
inexplicable miracles in their victory. Other miracles
took some thought to realize that they were miracles,
that the laws of nature were not the only thing at play
here. But anyone who saw what occurred in the Gulf
War saw openly that this was miraculous.

And yet people ask, "Where are the miracles today?"

52.

Lead a supernatural life and G-d will provide the
miracles.

ALL THE WORLD
IS MY TEACHER

The Baal Shem Tov taught that from every thing a person hears or sees in this world he must find a teaching in how Man should serve G-d. In truth, this is the whole meaning of service of G-d.

That was probably the most common opening to the Rebbe's talks. After all, the tzaddik doesn't see a world. He only sees and hears G-d teaching him.

53.

The great tzaddik, Rabbi Zusia of Anipoli, learned seven things from a thief:

1. A thief goes quietly. *So too, Zusia did not show off his accomplishments.*

2. A thief puts his life on the line to do what he has to do. *Zusia did the same to help a fellow human being.*

3. Every detail is crucial to a thief. *Zusia never overlooked any opportunity to do a good deed or learn from some experience.*

4. A thief works hard. *Zusia studied, prayed and meditated just as hard.*

5. A thief works efficiently. *Zusia never wasted precious time.*

6. A thief is optimistic and ever hopeful. *And so was Zusia.*

7. If the first attempt does not succeed, a thief will return to try again. *Zusia never gave up.*

54.

Even from the most horrible things we can learn great lessons. From the threat of nuclear destruction we can learn several things about how to rearrange the world for the good:

- You don't need great armies.
- It can take only one simple act.
- You don't have to understand how it works—just what button to press.
- It doesn't matter who does it, as long as he presses the right button.
- From the smallest things come the biggest changes.
- Tremendous power has always been there—it needs only be revealed.
- Since all this has only been discovered in our generation, it must be of particular relevance to us.

55.

Take-off of one of the Apollo missions was delayed due to a single, tiny loose component. From this the Rebbe learned:

The more momentous the mission, the more crucial the details.

Including the most momentous mission of all, the purpose of Creation.

56.

Let's say you are an astronaut, far beyond the earth on a very long journey. Let's say you get fed up with the constant barrage of instructions coming in on your radio from home base. So you shut it off. With no regrets. And you relax, enjoying the awesome scenery out the window. And time flies by...

But eventually, you realize you have no clue where you are. Or how to get back to where you want to be. And you remember that you had a mission, but you can quite get straight exactly what it was. You panic.

Finally, you remember the radio. You reactivate it. You hold the hand piece and call, "Home base? Astronaut calling home base! Answer me!!"

A faint reply is heard. It is the sweetest sound you've ever come by. Now you can get back on course.

We are all astronauts. We took off from Mount Sinai over 33 centuries ago with a plan to follow and a mission to accomplish. We've got to reconnect to our home base.

57.

In 1976, amidst multiple litigations, the multimillionaire, eccentric recluse, Howard Hughes, died. The Rebbe spoke about him:

He felt he could trust no one, for they were all only after his money. For the last twenty years of his life he could only hide from the entire world, without a friend, without any sort of enjoyment of life.

There was a man who had everything, and everything he had only locked him in.

He was like all of us. We hold the keys to our freedom, but we use them to lock ourselves in.

58.

My father-in-law, Professor Avraham Polichenco, was a professor of computer science in Argentina and introduced computers to Argentina in the 60s. At the same time he made a major shift in life, from an ardent secular Zionist with a bias towards anyone religious, to a fervent chassid with a keen interest in the Kaballa.

My father-in-law was privileged to have engaged the Rebbe in several long discussions. In one of those talks, they discussed computers. It is interesting that the Rebbe's concept of the computer back then in the 60s was very much the concept of "convergence" that only became popular in the early 90s.

What is new about the computer? You walk into a room and you see familiar machines: A typewriter, a tape recorder, a television, of course a calculator —but none of these are new.

Unseen, however, beneath the floors and behind the walls, are cables connecting all these machines to work together as one. There is a technology that allows them to all speak the same language —thereby transforming them from many ordinary machines into a single powerful computer.

Now, let's take your own life. You pray, you do business, you eat, you talk—each activity seemingly irrelevant to the next. A mess of fragments.

And such, too, is the native psyche of the human being: We have minds that understand one way, hearts that feels another—and what we do has often nothing to do with either of those.

Take the technology of the computer and apply it in terms of your everyday life: Find a common meaning at which all these fragments converge, and thereby unleash their power.

When a person wakes up in the morning and realizes he was created and placed here with a purpose, and that nothing in his life is irrelevant to that purpose, then all the fragments converge into one harmonious whole.

59.

On the first night of Chanuka all eight candle holders stand before you. But you light only one. Tomorrow night you shall light two. You know that eventually you will light all eight.

From which we learn two things:

1. Always grow. Always keep moving. If you did one good thing yesterday, do two today.

2. Move step by step in life. Take things on at a pace you can handle. Don't expect to become a tzaddik overnight. But never fool yourself that today's step means you have arrived.

60.

Why do you celebrate your birthday?

In your mother's womb, you were comfortable, warm and cared for. According to our sages, you learned there the entire Torah from an angel.

Then, you left. It was an ordeal, a trauma. The world you entered was cold and harsh. The mere act of living became a struggle. You cried.

Yet, every year you celebrate that day.

Because the day you were born was the day you became your own entity. No longer an extension of someone else. A proactive force in the world.

So celebrate your birthday. And take time to think: What have *I* given the world that was *not* given to me? Was I really born?

61.

The laser beam:

People have the wrong idea about restrictions: They imagine that if you restrict what you eat and what you do not, when you work and when you meditate and pray, what you wear, where you go—all these restrictions will suffocate any sense of inspiration.

The truth is, without any restrictions your inspiration will quickly dissipate. Focus your light like a laser into an intense, powerful beam and it will last.

62.

Electricity is a hidden force within the Creation. It cannot be grasped with any of the five senses—we can only know it from its effects and its causations. Yet from it we derive great light and power.

Electricity is a wonderful analogy for the mystical chassidic teachings.

63.

In recent years, astronomers have discovered that not all stars shine. There are some stars of such tremendous density that instead of radiating outwards, they only draw light in. Therefore, they have named these stars, "Black Holes".

Fortunately, the universe has enough Black Holes already. If you have light, shine forth.

64.

The body is not something to be abhorred or rejected. On the contrary, the body serves as sunglasses for the soul. Without the body, the soul can only perceive G-dliness in an abstract, ethereal way. The body allows the soul to stare straight into the face of G-dliness, in tangible, concrete terms.

Strange: We compare the Ultimate Being to a king, use parables of princes, brilliant jewels, birds, horses...yet what could all these have to do with the entirely abstract matters which they purport to represent? The Rebbe explained:

We and everything we see about us are but a reflection of that which is above. A king in our world is a reflection of the concept of Kingship above. The sweetness of a fruit is a reflection of the sweetness of the Supernal Wisdom. The form of the human body reflects the inner structure of the cosmos, so that each limb and organ parallels a particular Divine force.

Each of these things descends from its G-dly place into our material realm to take tangible form—so that we can grasp those G-dly concepts from which they extend. Even those inventions that only arose in the modern era were in fact hidden all this time within the Creation, waiting for us to discover them and reconnect them with their G-dly source and meaning.

MAKING A LIVING

After the Rebbe suffered a severe heart attack in his 75th year, he came back up from the depths—as you would expect from a tzaddik—holding brilliant new jewels of enlightenment. Wondrously, the jewels were not couched in the settings of the Rebbe's immediate world—a world of study, meditation and prayer—but in the story of one who struggles to retain spirituality while squeezing the world for a pay check (see 74.).

Those who had taken career advice from the Rebbe now realized how intimately the Rebbe lived with them in their struggle.

But why should a rebbe want to live—even vicariously—in a world of falsehood and blatant materialism?

Because when the world was made the most blinding sparks of light fell to the lowest places. So there, in the super-fragmented world of money and eeking out a living, there the Rebbe sees no dichotomy, nothing separate from G-d—only a grand purpose, a great mine in which to discover divine jewels of such value, they have never seen the light of day.

65.

It is written in the holy Zohar that those who have
their needs provided for today and sit and fret over
what will be tomorrow are not being practical—they
are simply incorrectly focussed.

Every day you are nourished straight from His full,
open and overflowing hand. Everything in between
—all your work and accounts and bills and receivables
and clientele and prospects and investments—all is
but a cloud of interface between His giving hand and
your soul, an interface of no real substance which He
bends and flexes at whim.

If so, if He is feeding you today, and He has fed you
and provided all you need and more all these days,
what concerns could you have about tomorrow? Is
there then something that could stand in His way?
Could He possibly have run out of means to provide
for you?

Take your focus off the measured channels by which
you receive and place your eyes on the Infinite Source
of Giving. The Source has no lack of channels.

66.

The reason you have a business is to reconnect all these fragments back to their Creator. And the gauge of your success is your attitude.

If you see yourself as a victim of circumstance, of competitors, markets and trends, that your bread is in the hands of flesh and blood...

...then your world is still something separate from your G-d.

But if you have the confidence that He is always with you in whatever you do and the only one who has the power to change your destiny is you yourself through your own acts of goodness...

...then your earth is tied to the heavens, and since in the heavens nothing is lacking, so too it shall be in your world.

67.

The common conception of how the system works is faulty. They see a career as *making a living*. A career doesn't *make* anything. What you receive is generated above, in a spiritual realm. Your business is to set up a channel to allow all that to flow into the material world.

68.

Every business is the business of a tailor: to make clothes for the blessings that come your way.

You can't alter the size of your blessings by putting them in bigger clothes—on the contrary, they might just be chased away. But neither must the clothes be too short. Because that is the whole purpose: that miracles and blessings should not come into the world stark naked, but be enclothed in the natural world. And we are the tailors.

69.

Joseph was imprisoned in Egypt. He knew there was purpose in his being there and that when the time came he would be released.

Eventually, it happened: The Pharaoh's cup-bearer asked Joseph to interpret his dream. Joseph thought, "This is the opportunity! This man is the means by which I shall be redeemed."

He interpreted the dream favorably, telling the cup-bearer he would soon be released. He then asked the man to return him the favor by pleading before Pharaoh on his behalf.

But when the dream was fulfilled, and the cup-bearer was released from prison, he promptly forgot Joseph for two years.

The wise men say that had Joseph not relied on the Egyptian, but solely on G-d alone, he would have been released two years earlier.

There is no person, no thing, no scheme upon which your livelihood or your fate rests. There is only the flow of blessing from Above.

True, that flow enclothes itself in tangible means, in job opportunities, in new clientele, in fresh markets, in well-connected acquaintances—but all these are only channels, not the source. Grasp any one of them and it may crumble in your hands.

Grasp the Source of Life.

70.

If you are an upright person then, "G-d will bless you in everything you do." Note, however, it says you must *do*.

We are meant to work through the processes of the material world. Why? Because this is the means by which the world is enlightened: the spiritual must invest itself into the mundane. And this can only be achieved by spiritual people working within the everyday world.

71.

Working for a living is good. G-d wants us to be involved in the material world in order to make it spiritual. What's *not* good are the *anxieties* over making a living.

Be within but stay above.

Don't let your inner self get involved in your business. That inner self must be preserved for fulfilling your purpose in life. Making lots of money is not your purpose in life.

72.

There is a raging storm at sea. There are hellish waves that crash and pound at the shore, carrying all away, leaving desolation behind.

The sea is the world of making a living. The waves are the stress and anxiety of indecision, not knowing which way to turn, on what to rely. Up and down, hot and cold—constantly churning back and forth.

Do as Noah did and build an ark.

An ark in Hebrew is "taiva"—which means also "a word". Your ark shall be the words of Torah and of prayer. Enter into your ark, and let the waters lift you up, rather than drown you with everything else.

73.

Every word of Torah is a story in your life, at every point of living.

First, Noah was told to enter the ark. Later he was told to leave the ark and enter a new world.

You must do both. First enter your ark, then leave to enter the world. If your ark was a real ark, then the world you will enter will not be the same world you just left.

74.

When the Mighty Waters cover your head, suffocating
the soul and the flame that burnt inside...

When raging torrents of confusion drag you away in
their current, ripping you from your hold on Life...

Look deeper. Beyond the soul.

For the soul itself, as well as the flame it holds, are
rooted in a serene G-dly World of Emanation, a world
of quietness and sublime harmony.

But the turbulence of this world is rooted even beyond
that, stemming from a World of Confusion, of light
unbounded and untamed, before the orderly
emanation of defined being,

> "—and the world was confused and void,
>   with darkness over the face of the deep."

So you must dig deeper than those roots, to find the
coals from which the flame arose and the flint rock
from which the spark was struck. Deeper, until you
reach the primordial essence of the soul, beyond
Emanation, beyond Light—even beyond the
unbounded light of pre-creation. Where there is
nothing but the seminal thought which inspired all
that is and was and will come to be.

And what was that thought? It was the thought of you
here and now, in your struggle with this world, and the
delicious taste of your victory.

And, since in that thought there is no past and future,
there, in that thought, you have already won.

Now you must make it happen.

75.

The river you travel will have its share of turbulence. It is an inevitable and inescapable ingredient of every river every man has ever travelled.

The choice is where you would like that turbulence. You can have it worrying about what path to take and what will be there and who to rely upon and what they will do to you and where you will go and what you should do when you get there...

Or you can stay above all that and fulfil your quota of turbulence as the Talmudic Master of Rogotchov did.

My teacher, Rabbi Yosef Rosen of Rogotchov, once confided that the Sabbath was the hardest day of his week. Every other day, when a thousand theories on a single page of Talmud would barrage into his mind, he could restrain them by writing. On the Sabbath, however, one is not allowed to write.

Everyone has his share of turbulence. You decide in which world yours should be.

76.

Ultimately, the waters cannot drown the soul, but only lift it above them—for, in truth, this is the purpose for which they were created.

77.

A meditation for when things get rough:

The world was brought into being with Goodness. And the ultimate good for Man is that he should not be shamed, but feel as a partner in the fulfillment of the Divine Plan. Free bread is to us bread of shame —such is the nature of Man.

That is why nothing good comes without toil. And according to the toil, can be known the harvest that will be reaped in the end.

78.

Depression, anxiety and pessimism damage the channels of blessing from Above.

These are the words of the Zohar:

"There is a lower world—our world—and there is a higher world.

"The lower world is meant to continuously receive from the higher world. But the higher world will only provide in accordance to the lower world's state of being.

"If the lower world glows with a luminous countenance, then it receives illumination from above. But if it wallows in depression and anxiety it receives strict judgement.

"Therefore it is written, "Serve G-d with joy!"

"And the joy of Man draws upon him another joy from above."

79.

There is no place for worry. You try to decide a course of action. If you do not have the experience to decide, ask the advice of someone who does—a parent, a teacher, an expert—someone reliable, but also someone who is conscientious of your spiritual path.

Once you have decided what should be done, you follow that course and you trust in G-d that since you are doing what you believe to be the right thing, He will insure that everything will go well.

80.

When things don't work out, trust in G-d and stay calm. Even if it's all your fault and you deserve everything you're getting, trust in G-d that it is all for the good, and stay calm.

When He sees how much you trust in Him, He will make it for the good.

81.

Two miracles, as related in the Babylonian Talmud and elaborated many times by the Rebbe:

On his travels, Rabbi Akiva took a donkey to free him from carrying his load, a rooster to wake him up early and a lamp to study by night. (The Rebbe would comment at this point that this is in contradistinction to the general custom today to take a credit card and a toothbrush.)

Rabbi Akiva was a great sage who taught, among other things, that everything the All-Merciful does is for the good.

Once the All-Merciful arranged for Rabbi Akiva to arrive at a walled town too late in the day, when the gates were already locked. He told himself it is all for the good and slept in the woods outside.

That night was full of disaster. When Rabbi Akiva sat down to study by the light of his lamp, a gust of wind blew it out. "Nu," he said, "everything is for the good"—and he lay down to sleep. After all, his rooster would wake him at the first hint of dawn.

But then, a fox attacked his rooster and ran off with it between his jaws. "Somehow," Rabbi Akiva said, "this is also for the good". And he fell asleep.

It was the middle of the night when the donkey ended up prey to a lion. Rabbi Akiva mourned for the donkey, but rejoiced at the great good that
—somehow, in some way—was being done for him.
And he fell back into a deep sleep.

In the morning he woke to find the town had been ransacked and burnt to the ground. "See," he said, "everything was for the good. Had I slept in the town, had my lamp burned, my rooster crowed or my donkey neighed, I would have been a target for the same pillagers that attacked that town!"

. . .

Rabbi Akiva saw it was *for* the good—but he did not see the good within the events themselves. He only saw that through these unfortunate events he was saved from an even more unfortunate one...

One of Rabbi Akiva's teachers was a man named Nachum of Gamzu. "Gam zu" was a place, but it also means "even this". Nachum always would repeat the words, "Even this is good."

Nachum, being an honest man, was chosen as the emissary of the Jews to present a chest of precious stones to the Caesar. All the way to Rome, Nachum guarded the chest with his life. But on the last leg of the journey, an innkeeper surreptitiously exchanged the precious stones for sand. By the time Nachum discovered the ploy, it was too late to turn back. So he happily exclaimed, "Even this is good! I shall do my job as emissary of the Jewish People, and G-d will fill in the rest!"— and continued his way to the Caesar.

"Your majesty, " he proclaimed before the royal throne, "The Jews send you a gift!" And he opened the chest of sand. Nobody was very impressed. When the Caesar had him thrown into a dungeon for his "mockery", Nachum joyously repeated his saying, "Even this is good!"

That's when the miracle occurred: One of Caesar's advisors (actually Elijah the Prophet in disguise) suggested that this sand may have magical powers. "After all," he explained, "the Jews have a legend that their forefather, Abraham, vanquished four kings and their armies using magical sand that turned into arrows when thrown."

The Caesar agreed—and the Romans had no lack of wars to experiment with. The sand was issued to the Roman legions fighting in Gaul, and before long, news of a great, miraculous victory was reported. Nachum was released and abundantly rewarded. He was delighted—but not the least bit surprised. He simply commented, "After all, everything is good. Had I brought jewels, the Caesar might have thrown them back in my face. But sand...!"

(By the way, the innkeeper got his own in the end. You see, when he got wind of the story, the poor fool also came to Rome, pulling a wagon load of his plain, ordinary sand for the Roman Legions...)

...

There are two paths: One: Everything is *for* the good. Perhaps not immediately, but eventually good will come out from it.

The other: Everything *is* truly good—because there is nothing else but He Who is Good. It's just a matter of holding firm a little longer, unperturbed by the phantoms of our limited vision, unimpressed by the paper tiger that calls itself a world, and eventually we will be granted a heart to understand and eyes to see. Eventually, it will become obvious good in our world as well.

Nachum of Gamzu was capable of revealing the innate good of every event in life—that the secret of each thing is truly good. And so, for him, it *was* that way.

82.

In every hardship, look for the spark of good and focus upon it with all your might. If you cannot find that spark, rejoice that wonder beyond your comprehension has befallen you.

Once you have unveiled and liberated the spark of good, it can rise to overcome its guise of darkness and even transform the darkness fully to light.

83.

Trusting in the One Above doesn't mean waiting for miracles.

It means having confidence in what you are doing right now—because you know He has put you on the right path and will fill whatever you do with divine energy and blessing from on high.

84.

You can read about G-d's involvement in this world in a book of philosophy. Or you can see it in real life in your business.

Look carefully, objectively, and you will realize that for you to make a living there must occur constant miracles, each greater than the miracle of the splitting of the Red Sea. The fact that you don't notice these miracles doesn't make them any less miracles. On the contrary, their loftiness transcends your perception.

85.

A good barometer to determine whether something will be of benefit materially, is whether it is the proper thing to do spiritually. A business venture that implies breaking your moral principles will also be detrimental materially.

At times, we experience tremendous pressure when our ethics seem to stand in the way of success—but this is only an illusion. The spiritual and the material are in conflict only to our subjective eyes. In fact, they work in harmony as one.

86.

Sometimes you see that things have been taken out of your hands and are following a supernatural order. At this point, just do your best at what you have to do—and stay out of G-d's way.

87.

Just as you search out a material career, so you must also search out a spiritual one. But there is a difference: With a material career you can only plow and sow and await the rains. With your spiritual career you must provide the rain as well—in other words, it is up to you to fill it with life.

88.

It's a paradox: The greatest revelations are to be found not in meditation, study and prayer, but in the mundane world—but only if you would rather be meditating, studying and praying.

89.

There was a chassid, Binyomin Klotzker, who dealt in timber. Once, he made his accounts for the day and on the bottom line he wrote, "There is nothing else but He."

When they demanded of him, "What are you doing meditating in the middle of business?" He explained, "If I can think business in the middle of meditating, I can meditate in the middle of business."

90.

There was a time when people did not have careers. People did not live to acquire material wealth.

People worked to earn enough for their families to eat that day, with a little extra saved for the Sabbath. Today we are slaves of the houses, the cars and the gadgets we must acquire.

...

Rabbi Shalom Ber of Lubavitch had a chassid who owned a boot-making business. Seeing how this chassid had become obsessed with his business, he commented, "Feet in galoshes I've seen. A head in galoshes I've never seen before."

When wall-to-wall carpeting came in vogue in the fifties and everyone had to take a bank loan to have them, the Rebbe retold this episode and concluded,

"At least boots are higher than the ground. But heads into carpets...!"

91.

The natural tendency is to treat matters of the spirit as luxury items—sort of an appendage to life. Eating, sleeping, making money—these things are given priority over all and the time dedicated to them is sacrosanct. But prayer, meditation and study fit in only when you feel like it, and are pushed aside on the slightest whim.

You've got to make your priorities faithful to your inner self. You've got to ask yourself if this is what your life is all about.

Set a schedule for spiritually enriching activities. Be as tough with that schedule as a workaholic would be with his business.

92.

In truth, there are two possible channels by which to receive your livelihood, according to the perspective you take in life:

You could decide to become just another element of nature, chasing after your bread in the chaos, running the race of survival of the fittest.

And the fact is, you *may* even do well taking this route—in the short run. In the long run, however, your soul is being denied its nourishment, and your body, too, will never feel satisfied.

Or you could see your life as an intimate relationship with the Source of Life Above—as though all your livelihood was no more than manna from heaven, handed to you personally and lovingly straight from the hand of your G-d and partner in all you do.

Then your main job is to keep the basket where your manna will fall sparkling clean, insuring that no one is being hurt or misled by your business. To spend the profits you are granted on spreading kindness in the world.

Maybe you'll get rich this way. Maybe you won't. But you will always be satisfied.

93.

Take G-d as a partner in your business. Offer Him 10% of all net profits and He won't refuse.

94.

To a mother who asked advice on becoming a typist to supplement the family income:

Don't become a typist. You are a mother. Type, if you feel you need to in order to support your family. But don't *become* a typist.

Be within, but stay above

STRUGGLE

It is one of the most ingenious innovations of chassidic thought: Even if you fail to conquer the darkness entirely, even if you are still rolling in the mud with the enemy—you can still find G-d in the struggle itself.

It's just another corollary of the one basic thought: There is no place where He is not.

95.

The angels are jealous of he who struggles in darkness.
They have light, but he touches the Essence.

96.

Everyone has his share of "not good". It's impossible
that a physical being should be void of faults. The
point is not to flee or hide from them. Nor is it to
resign yourself to it all. It is to face up to the fact that
they are there, and to systematically chase them away.

Recognizing who you are and gradually cleaning up
your act—it may look ugly, but it is a divine path.

97.

You cannot blame yourself, never mind persecute
yourself for how you feel. But you can rejoice in the
battle of controlling and sublimating those feelings.
Every small victory within yourself is a major triumph
over the darkness of this world. Indeed, this is why this
darkness was placed within you, in order that you may
transform it into great light.

98.

There are times when the most destructive impulses within us come dressed in a prayer shawl.

When it is time to rejoice, and a voice tells you to feel remorse over your sins.

When it is time for remorse, and it tells you, "Who do you think you are, that you should feel remorse?"

When there is someone who desperately needs your help and you decide it is time to meditate.

When it is time to meditate, and you decide you must go out to save the world.

When you have attained a grasp of a deep concept, or prayed to G-d with great fervor, or secretly performed a beautiful deed—and a voice inside says, "Boy, are you good!"

There is only one thing that voice inside will never tell you to do and will only do everything it can to obstruct. It will never say to break the chains with which it has bound you and change yourself.

99.

The world is not a reasonable place. Meet it on its own terms: When you do something good, do it beyond reason.

...

This is how that darkness within us finds its way out: First it agrees with everything good we do.

When we choose to meditate, it tells us, "Yes! Meditate! That way you will become a great sage!"

When we choose to do a good deed, it says, "Yes! You are so wonderful! Think what others will do in return for this!"

Slowly, slowly, it convinces us that any good we do requires its approval. And then, you've fallen into its trap.

Do good without reason. Then there are no traps.

100.

Mockery is the prime weapon of the dark impulses within Man. It is the prime obstacle to moving forward and upward—the thought that perhaps people will say, "Why are you behaving today differently than you did yesterday? Weren't you good enough then? Are you really so great today?"

And the most powerful mocker is the one within your own self.

When you start something you know is good and right, and you hear a voice inside saying, "Hold it! Who do you think you are to take on such a lofty noble path? Hypocrite! Don't you remember what you were involved in just a moment ago?"

— know that what you did a moment ago is irrelevant. All that matters is what you will do right now.

Any voice that comes to prevent you from progressing forward—no matter how justified its case may be—any such voice is a voice of destruction and decay, not of growth and life.

101.

There is always hope. Even when you mess up, you have not wrestled control from Him. After all the dust has settled, where you are and how you are is exactly as He had planned at the outset of creation.

And so, there is always hope.

102.

Every moment, every human activity is an opportunity to connect with the Infinite. Every act can be an uplifting of the soul. It is only your will that may stand in the way. But as soon as you wish, you are connected.

103.

Fasting and punishing the body is not a path for our generation. Not only because most of us are too fragile to weaken our bodies any more. Not only because the faintness of hunger can interfere with your ability to do good in the world. But principally because now has come the time to lead a spiritual life *with* the body rather than against it.

104.

Remember you are not the body. Neither are you the animal that pounds within the body, demanding its way in every thing. You are a G-dly soul.

Do not confuse the pain and struggle of the body with the joy and purity of the G-dly soul.

105.

Advice on anger:

Prepare yourself with this meditation, and when you feel anger overcoming you, run through it in your mind:

Know that all that befalls you comes from a single source, that there is nothing outside of that Oneness to be blamed for any event in the universe. There is no other force but G-d.

And although this person who insulted you, or hurt you, or damaged your property—he is granted free choice and is held culpable for his decision to do wrong—

That is *his* problem. That it had to happen to *you* —that is *your* problem.

All of your world is G-d speaking to you. Listen carefully.

106.

There are times when everything about you, the entire world in all its chutzpah, denies the truth you know within.

There are times you must be a lion, a deer, an eagle, a tree—but now you must be a rock.

Now you must not flinch, not in any way even acknowledge the existence of the mighty waves that come crashing down upon you, conspiring to grind you to sand, to sweep you away to join them in the vast ocean.

You must be the hard, unmoving rock that lies at the essence of your soul, the voice from beyond all this ephemeral reality, from beyond all time and space, that says, "They are nothing. There is none else but He."

It begins with you. And then it happens in your world: The outer crust of facade begins to crack, the essential reality is revealed, the storm dissipates as though it never were, and all things begin to say, "I am not a thing. In truth, there is none else but He."

107.

There are sparks of light hidden in this world. Some you can find and liberate: When you "Know G-d in all your ways"—finding Him in whatever you do, those sparks jump out at you and their light is released.

But then there are sparks of such intensity that they had to be buried in the deepest bowels of the material realm and locked away in thick darkness. These are sparks that no ordinary search could uncover: Your intellect has no power even to approach them. Your deeds could never dig that deep. Your eyes would be blinded by their brilliance and by the profundity of the darkness surrounding them.

The only tools you have to liberate those sparks are the ones that supersede your intellect and your senses. These are the inner powers that are revealed when you withstand a test of faith.

This is the reason we find our faith tested again and again in this generation: We are redeeming the final sparks of light.

108.

Isn't this the whole meaning of life in this world—to choose between connecting to the material world and believing that your life comes from those many forces, or to choose true life and to believe that all your needs and all your concerns come only from the One G-d of Life?

109.

Many woman who asked the Rebbe's advice in choosing a Hebrew name for themselves were told, "Choose the name 'Malka' ('Queen'), and become a ruler over yourself."

. . .

You are the master over the animal within, not the slave. Just because it burns inside like a furnace doesn't mean you must obey.

110.

Elijah, the prophet, rebuked his people. "How long will you walk on both sides of the fence?" he demanded. "Decide now! Either you are for the idolatry of Baal, or you are for the One Living G-d!"

Now didn't Elijah think, "Just a minute! What will happen if they choose the first option? Won't it be all my fault?"

No, he didn't. He knew his people better than that. He knew if they were pushed up against the wall and given an ultimatum to choose either/or, they would make the right choice.

So why do we grab for the wrong things in life? Because we fool ourselves into thinking we can have it all. All the darkness and all the light in one package.

We can't.

111.

When Isaiah informed King Chizkia of the heavenly decree that he would die, the king replied, "I have a tradition from my ancestor, David: Even when the sword is drawn over your neck do not refrain from pleading for mercy from Above."

There is hope, and there is trust in G-d—and they are two distinct attitudes.

Hope is when there is something to latch on to, some glimmer of a chance. The drowning man, they say, will clutch at any straw to save his life.

Trust in G-d is even when there is nothing in which to hope. The decree is sealed. The sword is drawn over the neck. By all laws of nature there is no way out.

But the One who runs the show doesn't need any props.

112.

If you are confident that G-d will help you, then why is misery and anxiety written all across your face? If you are really confident, celebrate!

STRUGGLE

FROM DESPAIR
TO JOY

Describing the joy of the Rebbe is something like describing the majesty of the Rocky Mountains to a prairie dweller. We think of happiness as all the outer trappings of smiley faces and the "having-a-good-time" look. But what we saw on the Rebbe was an inner joy—the sort you feel when a sudden, brilliant light bulb flashes inside—except continual and constant. Not a joy that dissipates and burns itself out, but a tightly contained joy of endless optimism, power and life, waiting the special moment when it would burst forth like an unexpected tsunami, sweeping up every soul in its path.

Even now, if you would enter the Rebbe's private office (it's possible with some effort), you would feel there the vitalizing joy that pervades the air and every object the Rebbe touched.

The Rebbe once confided that he himself was by nature a somber and introspective person. With hard work, he said, he was able to affect his spirit to be full of joy.

113.

Many who wrote to the Rebbe of their despair received an answer similar to the following:

Despair is the diametric opposite of everything in which we believe—in other words: it is a denial of reality.

It is a denial that there is a G-d who directs all of His creation and watches over every individual and assists each one in what he must accomplish…

114.

Depression is not a crime. But it plummets a person into an abyss deeper than any crime could reach.

Nevertheless, there were those who the Rebbe also advised to seek medical help.

Depression is a ploy instigated by the self-destructive elements within all of us. Once depressed, a person could do anything.

Fight depression as a blood sworn enemy. Run from it as you would run from death itself.

115.

Despair is the ultimate form of self-worship—the perception that you have the capacity to truly mess up, to take the world's destiny out of its Creator's hands and sabotage His plans.

Know that the world is in a constant state of elevation, rocketing upwards towards its ultimate wholeness at every moment. Every quivering of every leaf, every subtle breeze, every slightest motion of any particle of our universe is another move in that same direction. Even those events that seem to thrust downward are in truth only a part of the ascent—like the poise of an athlete before he leaps, the contraction of a spring before its energy is released.

There is not a thing you could do halt that dynamic even for a moment. True, you must take responsibility for your deeds and work hard, very hard, to clean up your own mess. But when all the dust settles, you are exactly in the space where you were meant to be: One step closer.

116.

Between a cold spirit and G-dlessness lies a flimsy partition.

Man must serve with a heart of fire.

117.

There are many kinds of barriers: Those from within and those from without. Barriers between people. Barriers that prevent you from doing good things. Barriers of your own mind and your own hesitations. There are the barriers that exist simply because you are a limited being.

Joy breaks through all barriers.

118.

You ask, "How can I be happy if I am not?"

True, you can't control the way you feel, but you do have control over your conscious thought, speech and actions. Do something simple: Think good thoughts, speak good things, behave the way a joyful person behaves—even if you don't fully feel it inside. Eventually, the inner joy of the soul will break through.

119.

You write that, having discovered all your faults, you are depressed.

Imagine you have just found a doctor with a diagnosis that explains all your afflictions over the past many years. And he's written a prescription directing you on a sure path to good health. Shouldn't you jump with joy and relief?

120.

Much depression stems from haughtiness. If you would realize who you really are, you wouldn't be so disappointed with yourself.

121.

You must always have good things to think about. An empty mind is a vacuum awaiting destructive thoughts.

...

Where your thoughts are— that is where you are, all of you.

Try to be always in good places.

122.

If you think about yourself all day, you are guaranteed to become depressed. Take an hour a day to think of how you can benefit someone else.

...

Complacency breeds anxiety. To be healthy, a person needs to be affecting his surroundings, uplifting those about him and bringing in more light.

123.

Despair is a cheap excuse for avoiding one's purpose in life. And a sense of purpose is the best way to avoid despair.

124.

To a young man who wrote he lacked self-confidence in dealing with others:

Sit with friends and work together with friends. Soon you will see you can do as well as them. Then the inner strength of your soul will begin to shine through.

125.

Everything that occurs comes from Him, and He is only good. But if you and your world are not prepared to receive such good, it may manifest itself as apparent bad. Struggle hard to see the good, think positively—and then the good will become revealed.

126.

The natural state of Man, the way G-d created him, is to be happy. Look at children and you will see.

127.

Everything must be done with joy. Even remorse can be with joy.

...

People imagine a place of G-dliness as serious, awesome and intrepidating. That fact is, where G-d is, there is joy.

That is why our every moment is a moment to celebrate and fill with joy. Because at every moment we are fulfilling our mission of bringing G-dliness into this world. Not just the obviously joyful matters, such as meditation, study, prayer and good deeds, but also regular, mundane activities and the ways we earn an income and go about life—all are ways by which we know Him and bring Him into our world.

And where there is G-d, there is strength and joy.

128.

A person is happy when he knows something worthwhile belongs to him. A person is very happy when he feels he is small and yet he owns something very great.

We are all finite owners of the Infinite.

129.

The chassidic master, Rabbi Meir of Premishlan lived at the foot of a steep hill. Every day, even in the winter snow and ice, he would hike over the hill to immerse and purify his body in a brook on the other side. The people considered this quite wondrous, since others could only walk around the hill—no one dared to challenge the ice.

Until a few young men decided to put an end to this superstition. They brazenly followed Rabbi Meir as he effortlessly ascended the hill.

All of them fell and were badly hurt.

What was Rabbi Meir's secret?

"When you are connected to Above," he explained, "you don't fall down."

130.

When I first showed this book to friends I detected a disdain for the phrase "serving G-d"—a concept that comes up so often. After all, servitude went out of fashion with the Emancipation.

But I left the term in. After all, this is not a book about friends' thoughts or even my own thoughts—this is about the Rebbe, and that's the term he used.

Servitude conjures a sense of surrendering one's being to another entity—thereby imprisoning all the potential of self fulfillment you've been given. But when we talk about serving the very source of your being, the surrender of self takes on a whole new and opposite meaning.

In your source, you are infinite—as your Creator is infinite. Serving your Creator then reads as plugging in to the ultimate self, becoming one with the infinite, one with the Creator Himself.

...

The purpose of every human being is to serve his Creator, and that is a service of great joy:

"I, puny mortal and decidedly finite being, serve with my deeds the Infinite Creator of All Worlds! I am bound to the Source of Life from birth, and all the many raging waters of this world cannot tear me away from that bond. Even if I sometimes fail, I may always return and in a single moment reconnect all my soul."

From Despair to Joy

BRICK WALLS

In the yard of the Rebbe's childhood home was a large tree. The Rebbe's mother related that when her son was five years old, he climbed to the top of the tree. She called up to him, "Mendel! Why is it that all the other children who climb this tree fall down, but you made it all the way up?"

Her son replied, "They look down and get nervous and fall, but I look only up and when you look only up, you don't fall down."

Why is it that the great masters move forward and upward with such invincible confidence, that they know no fear of man or thing, that mountains melt before their word?

Certainly, it is their clarity of vision. We who sleep when we are awake, are awake when we sleep, believe but do not believe, know but do not realize—we can never allow ourselves to walk straight into the light, because we are never sure it is not darkness. When we step forward we look behind us, when we go up we are looking below.

But the tzaddik's vision is sharp and clear. His words are solid and firm, his conviction will pierce a mountain. He sees no obstacles in his path—only the light that draws him.

131.

It is a Jewish Custom on the holy day of Rosh Hashana to walk to a pond or river and recite certain prayers there.

In Brooklyn, finding such a body of water within walking distance can be a bit of a problem. In the early years of the Rebbe's leadership, there would be a whole parade every year to the Brooklyn Botanical Gardens, attended by all the chassidim, with the Rebbe at the head.

One year, the rain poured incessantly and most assumed the walk cancelled. "Cancelled", however, was never part of the Rebbe's vocabulary. When the Rebbe came out for the walk, news travelled like lighting and people scrambled to join. Upon arrival at the gardens, however, they found the gates locked and nobody there to let them in.

The wall around the Brooklyn Botanical Gardens is fairly high. The Rebbe gazed up and said softly to his assistant, "How tall do you think that wall is?"

The assistant had no time to answer. The Rebbe was already climbing the wall.

As soon as they realized what was going on, chassidim rushed to assist the Rebbe. He looked down and said, "If you will allow me to do this myself, I think I will be far more successful."

That was the day the walls of the Brooklyn Botanical Gardens were breached by hundreds of chassidim.

It was also a day the chassidim learned the Rebbe meant what he preached.

Literally.

...

Rabbi Shmuel of Lubavitch, known as "The Rebbe Maharash", the fourth in the golden chain of rebbes of Lubavitch, had an attitude.

Many wise people say if you can't go under, go over. The Rebbe Maharash said, "Just go over."

Meaning that instead of first trying to work through a problem by its own rules, and then—if that doesn't work—gathering the strength and courage to step brazenly over it...

Instead, just start by stepping right over it, as though there were no obstacle to begin with.

After all, that's why obstacles are there—in order to lift you higher.

132.

On their exodus from Egypt, towards Mount Sinai, the Jewish People arrived at an obstacle—the Red Sea. They divided into four parties.

One prepared to fight.

One said to surrender and return.

One advocated mass suicide.

One began to pray.

G-d spoke to Moses and said, "Why are you crying out to me? I told you to travel straight ahead. Keep going and you will see there is no obstacle!"

The Jewish People kept going and the obstacle became a miracle.

133.

People think that G-d first made a world and then gave
us instructions to follow, so we won't mess it up. The
truth is, the instructions came first, and the world was
designed as the venue to carry them out.

Therefore, to say that anything in the world could be
an opposition to carrying out its Creator's will is an
absurdity. There can be no opponents to the purpose
of creation—only meaningful challenges.

134.

Hardships in life are the material world's way of
beckoning to you, "Purify me! Elevate me!" They come
to you knowing you can withstand them, and thereby
they will fulfill their purpose of being.

135.

Life's challenges are isometrics for the soul. They force
out its inner powers.

136.

Don't take the world and its darkness so seriously
—it is not as real as it feigns to be. It is only a creation
and it is being re-created out of absolutely nothing at
every moment. The only thing *real* about it is its
purpose of being—that you should purify it.

137.

This world operates on chutzpah. It has the chutzpah to declare itself a world, to assert that it is autonomous from its Creator, to deny any relationship to the very force that is continually bringing it into being every moment.

We will fight chutzpah with chutzpah.

138.

In Hebrew, the word for *world* is עולם *(olam)* and the word for *concealment* is העלם *(hellem)*. The two are closely related. The world exists only by virtue of concealing its true identity. It pretends to be your opposition, but in truth it's rooting for you.

. . .

It knows its deepest treasures can only be revealed by the deepest powers of your soul, and it taps those powers by challenging you.

139.

There's no such thing as defeat. There's always another chance. To believe in defeat is to believe that there is something, a certain point in time that did not come from Above.

Know that G-d doesn't have failures. If things appear to worsen, it is only as part of them getting better. We only fall down in order to bounce back even higher.

140.

Adam was the direct handiwork of G-d. No other human being could ever be as magnificent. Yet he had only one temptation to resist and he gave in.

Which teaches us that the greatest challenges in life are those that are closest to one's purpose of being. To the point that if you wish to know your central purpose in life, you need only look at where your greatest challenges are.

141.

Your soul is in captivity when you know what is right, but you allow the world to stop you.

For example, say you are the leader of a country. You decide what is the right thing to do, and you begin to do it. The newspapers, of course, condemn you. Your own people tell you you've made a mistake. You are being called wicked, immoral and compared to the worst villains of history. The United Nations convenes to unanimously protest your actions. The President of the United States calls you up to tell you to stop or forego further financial and military support.

But you know what you are doing is right. If you give in, your soul is in captivity.

142.

Captivity begins by believing that you are small and the world is big.

Once you believe that, next you are likely to believe it will step on you, and you fear it.

And then you come to obey it, then to run after it. And then you are it's slave, thirsting for water for the soul but not even able to remember where to look for it.

To fear the world is to deny the Oneness of its Creator.

143.

When the spies that Moses sent returned from their rendezvous of the Land of Canaan, they included in their report these words:

"We felt like ants before them, and so we were in their eyes."

Because they felt like ants in their own eyes, therefore, others saw them as ants as well.

144.

One who really cares is not placated by the fact that he has a good excuse.

If the goal was not achieved, it was not achieved —regardless of the excuse.

145.

Sometimes it may appear that there is a place where, according to all considerations, G-dliness can't come. An obstacle that prevents you from accomplishing something beneficial. A friend who cannot be approached to help do a favor. A gathering of people that seems meaningless.

The appropriate thing to do in such a situation is to throw out all considerations and just *do*. Your job is not to determine *if* and *where*. Your job is to determine *how*. Do, and you will see miracles.

146.

To one who fell into enormous debt trying to achieve miracles:

We were told to transcend limitations—but that doesn't mean just jumping into the air with no idea of where you're going to land!

COMING HOME

*In the Rebbe's spiritual universe, there are no strangers to the
Source of Life. It is not a place that is discovered, or that you
come to as a tourist. There is only return. Reconnection.*

*The soul begins in an intimate, essential bond with a Source
Beyond All Things. Even as she invests herself into a material
world, into a human form, that primordial bond remains
imprinted deep within her. It is that bond that pulls her constantly
to return, like a magnet pulling its lost other half. All the searching
of Man, all his spiritual striving, all is only an expression of this
dynamic, this thirst to return.*

*The desire to return is innate, but it must be awakened. The soul
must first realize she is distant. Return in all its strength and
passion is found, therefore, in the soul who has wandered far
from her true self and then awakened to recognize she is lost*

*As well, the drive to return is G-d's fishing net. For in its search to
reunite with Him, the soul finds G-d in all the matters of this
world. And so, these too are pulled in. And the deeper the descent,
the greater the treasure.*

147.

Our world is a world where a rainbow could be.

At first, there was a world that only received and returned no dividends. Its inhabitants took no ownership. They lived with their Creator's benevolence, they did what they did with no need for excuses, and eventually died as they died. And that was it.

With the Flood, this world was re-created. The earth was cleansed, the atmosphere purified. It became a world that could take the sunshine that poured in from above and refract it into many colors.

It became a world where a created being could be born, take the soul, body, share of the world and all the sustenance its Maker gave to it, *use* that, *do something* with that—and then return it, saying, "See what I have done with what you gave me!"

And so, G-d vowed to never destroy the world again. For, if the inhabitants would go wrong, they might always turn around and clean up their own mess.

148.

An ancient *Midrash* (with embellishment):

Adam trudged past the gates of Eden, his head low, his feet heavy with remorse and pain.

Then he stopped. A thought had struck him.

He spun around, looked up and exclaimed, "Wait a minute! You had this all planned! You put that fruit there knowing I would eat from it! This is all a plot!

"And I can prove it: In your Torah which You composed before the world was created, You wrote, "This is what should be done with a man when he dies…"

"So You had planned death should be in the world! You only wanted it should enter on *my* account!"

The Midrash does not record any retort to Adam's cry. Only silence.

G-d saw the soul of Man that it was very great and He asked, "How will all this greatness be realized?"

And so, he allowed Man free choice—to choose his own victories or to make his own blunders.

Without failure, Man will never truly reach into the depths of his soul. Only once he has failed, can he return and reach higher and higher without end. Beyond Eden.

149.

I push my child on the swing, and she returns. The harder I push, the higher she returns.

Success, in the higher scheme of things, is when a soul that has alienated herself returns. It is the ultimate demonstration of her resilience and her depth: No matter how distant she may travel, in the end she can never tear herself away.

150.

Return is the ultimate act of self expression. Nobody returns because he is commanded to do so. The ability to return comes from you alone.

And that itself the evidence that you were never truly torn away: The outer garments of the soul may have been severed, but the core remained at every moment in intimate union with its Source. And from there came the message to return.

151.

We came here that we may experience return. It is the ultimate experience.

One who returns from the darkness must bring of it with him and convert it to light. He must exploit his experience to surge higher and higher with greater strength.

Therefore, the one who returns from a distance is greater than the one who was always close. What matters is not so much where you stand, but with what force you are moving in which direction.

152.

In creating the whole of existence, G-d made forces that reveal Him and forces that oppose Him—He made light and He made darkness. One who does good brings in more light. One who fails, feeds the darkness.

But the one who fails and then returns transcends that entire scheme. He reaches out directly to the Essential Creator. Beyond darkness and light.

And so, his darkness becomes light.

...

When light pushes away the darkness, eventually another darkness shall come.

When the darkness itself is transformed into light, it is a light that no darkness can oppose.

153.

To return takes but a moment. One moment a being is at an ultimate distance from her G-d and from her true self, the next she is in complete union. The power to return is beyond time.

He did everything so we could not find our way home. So we flew afar to quench our thirst with foreign waters.
Now we return with a passion, clutching the Divine sparks we discovered on our journey.
We are His homing pigeons.

HEALING

HEALING

Hundreds of letters arrived daily to the Rebbe asking for advice and blessing in medical matters. That there were miracles is undisputed. Gather together ten Jews anywhere in the world and one will have a story about a friend, a relative or perhaps his or her own self to whom a miracle of the Rebbe occurred.

But the Rebbe didn't want to make a religion out of miracle healing. With almost every response, he gave practical advice, generally encouraging people along a spiritual path together with a wise medical one. Here are a few of the more typical responses:

154.

People think that if they are not well, they must
sacrifice all meaning in their life in order to take care of
their physical situation. In fact, the opposite is true:
You cannot separate the healing of the body from the
healing of the soul. As you treat the body, you must
also *increase* in nourishing the soul. Doctors know
this very well, but they should make better use of the
fact.

155.

To serve G-d you need a healthy body as well as a
healthy soul. How can you meditate, pray or study
properly when the body's wellness is neglected?
Taking care of your body so that the soul can flourish
is a divine service.

156.

Don't be so upset with the world. Anger at the world is
anger at G-d, and it's also bad for your blood pressure.

157.

Ask the advice of a doctor who is a friend. Being a
friend makes a big difference.

158.

In general, when doctors disagree, follow the opinion of the majority of the experts. But in the case of surgery, if there is uncertainty it is usually better to refrain and trust that the Healer of All Flesh will heal and strengthen you.

159.

Firm confidence in G-d can perform miracles of healing. Nevertheless, you should still follow the instructions of the doctor.

Not that it is the doctor or his medicine that heals —it is the Healer of All Flesh who heals. But the doctor and the medicine provide a natural channel for the healing to occur, and this is the way G-d prefers His miracles to work—through natural means.

...

Four things advised for healing:

1. Find a good doctor and follow his instructions.

2. Dispel any thoughts about illness. Think only healthy thoughts.

3. Strengthen your confidence in the Healer of All Flesh, that He will heal you in whatever way He sees fit.

4. Increase your study of the inner light of Torah.

160.

The doctor has been licensed from Above to heal, not to make predictions. Ignore the predictions and think only good thoughts.

BREAKING FREE

In Russia, for 70 years, the life of a chassid was a perpetual act of martyrdom. Leading your life the way you knew it was supposed to be led meant carrying the weight of the Kremlin and the KGB ominously over your head, with the constant threat of arrest, torture and exile to Siberia. It meant every week risking another strategy to avoid work on Saturday, teaching your children in a different secret cellar each day, suffering scorn and ridicule for being who you were.

Then they came to America. And they could not find the enemy.

It is not a problem unique to chassidim, but to Jews in general who migrated to a new world and just couldn't see the connection between all this and what they had left behind. And the same applies with every lifestyle that ever hit these shores—how do you pass on to the next generation something that doesn't seem to fit in this new context even for yourself?

This is a task where the human mind finds great difficulty: Relating familiar ideas to a new, completely unfamiliar time and place. We are dragged helplessly by the current of Time, mercilessly ripped from our hold on the past that fathered us, forcibly confronting a future with no chance to prepare. We are the intimated victims, servants and prisoners of Time, forever bowing to the pressures of the moment.

But then there are souls that remain beyond the realm of time and place, even while they enter into it. They know Time as one who looks down from the highest mountain, watching as snow becomes creek becomes river becomes sea. To them there is no dissonance, no conflict—only the movements of a magnificent symphony.

Into our time entered the Rebbe.

Those who could see no further than their own optic nerve saw the Rebbe as a relic of the past. With an untainted eye it was obvious that to the Rebbe there is no past.

To others, life in the small Jewish settlements of Europe had no relevance to the new life in America. Chassidism was quaint—a nice thing in another century—but not for now. The Rebbe saw the essence of that life, and the essence doesn't change.

To others, the time and place of martyrdom had ended, and an era of freedom and self-indulgence had begun. To the Rebbe, it is all just a newer and even higher rung on the ladder of transcendence of the self.

161.

The last written work of the Rebbe before his stroke centered on the following thought. The Rebbe personally handed a copy to thousands of his chassidim. I believe it is a summary of who we are and what we must do:

Self sacrifice in a land of freedom penetrates to the bone.

I saw men and women who sacrificed all they had to withstand the religious persecution of the Bolshevik regime. They came to a land of freedom and comfort and where is their greatness now?

A person is bred in that land of freedom and comfort, worshipping it, chasing after it—but inside he is crushed by the spiritual void. His inner being does not let him alone, the spark inside that cries, "This is not what I really want! I don't want this world! I don't want any worlds! All I want is Him alone!"

This is the crushing of an olive for its oil. The oil spreads and penetrates every fibre of his being. He is lit by the tzaddik and now his every faculty begins to burn. And there shines the source of light that can never be extinguished nor dimmed.

This is the light of Moshiach.

162.

They think self surrender means to say, "I have no mind. I have no heart. I only believe and follow, for I am nothing."

This is not self surrender, this is denial of the truth. For it is saying there is a place where G-dliness cannot be—namely your mind and your heart.

G-d did not give you a brain that you should abandon it, or a personality that you should ignore it. These are the building materials from which you may forge a sanctuary for Him, to bring Divine Presence into the physical realm.

Don't run from the self G-d has entrusted you with. Connect your entire being to its Essential Source. Permeate every cell with the light of self surrender.

163.

Great things are not what is demanded from our generation. The previous generations did all that for us. We need only do the small things—but in a more difficult time.

For us, self sacrifice could mean nothing more than a simple change of habit.

164.

Self surrender doesn't mean jumping off a bridge. Self surrender means surrendering the self. Putting aside the "I want", the "I need", the "I think such-and-such". Even the "I am".

Self surrender is the subliminal drive behind all authentically good deeds. But as the world becomes more materialistic and the challenges greater, the self-surrender can no longer stay so subliminal.

165.

Confidence is best found among the truly humble.

Moses was the most humble of all men. Yet he had the confidence to stand before the mightiest dictator on earth and assert his demands. He had the confidence to stand before G-d and listen without losing his composure. He had the confidence even to argue with G-d, when necessary.

Yet he considered himself to be nothing.

The confidence of Moses was not confidence in his own self. He had no self. He was but an agent of Above. Above there is infinite power.

Self-confidence is limited, at best. But if you trust in the One who has sent you to be here and do what you need to do—that confidence knows no bounds.

166.

Humility has to be real. Real humility means transcendence of the self.

Moses, it is written, was the most humble of all men. Obviously, he knew who he was. He knew that of all men, he alone was chosen to accomplish the greatest tasks of history—to lead an entire nation out from bondage and bring them to the greatest revelation that would ever be. He was the loftiest of all prophets, who spoke directly to G-d whenever he wished. He knew all this and yet he was humble.

Because Moses told himself, "This is not my own achievement. This is what I have done with the powers G-d has granted me. Perhaps had someone else been given these same powers, perhaps that someone else would have done a better job."

167.

Man is G-d's needle to sew the many patches of Creation into a single garment for His glory.

At one end, the needle must be hard and sharp, to squeeze through the ordeal. But the other end must have a vacant hollow, a nothingness with which to hold the thread.

With the world, we are firm and sharp. Within, we know we are nothing before the Infinite.

168.

One who feels himself cannot feel joy.

True happiness is the highest form of self sacrifice. There, in that state, there is no sense of self—not even an awareness that you are happy. True happiness is somewhere beyond "knowing". Beyond self.

All the more so when you bring joy to others.

169.

A sense of nothingness doesn't mean being everybody's doormat. In fact, just the opposite: A sense of nothingness is your gateway to infinite powers.

This is what is written in the Zohar:

Said the Master of the Academy of the Garden of Eden, "Whoever is small, is big. But whoever is big, is small."

Make yourself small and you will be greater.

Know you are nothing and you will be infinite.

At the very least, don't make such a big deal of yourself.

And you will be all that much closer to the truth.

170.

We are all prisoners. But we sit on the keys.

...

Finitude is our cell. The universe is our prison. Our jailkeeper is the Act of Being.

The keys to liberation are clenched tight in the fists of our own egos.

171.

The primordial blunder was the discovery of self.

The first man and woman in the Garden of Eden ate of the Tree of Knowledge and realized that they exist. Ever since then, that self-consciousness has been the root of every disaster.

Every "I" and "me", every sense of being is a denial of the Oneness of the Creator and the creation. It is a statement that there is something else, namely *me*, and I am autonomous from all this.

The goal of mankind is to reach beyond the state of Adam and Eve in the Garden—to a state where any sense of ego is meaningless. A place called Eden which is beyond the Garden, the place of Essential Being from where all delights flow... "And a river went out from Eden to water the Garden."

And now you know why they ate of the fruit to begin with.

172.

The biblical slavery of Egypt represents bondage to your own self.

Every day, at every moment, must be an exodus from the self. If you're not leaving Egypt, you're already back there.

173.

The ancient philosophers divided the world into four realms, each realm transcendental in a way beyond those that precede it:

inanimate = sounds

flora = emotions

fauna = intellect

human = dialogue

The inanimate—earth, rocks, water, etc., do not transcend their bounds in any way.

Flora transcends its bounds by growing.

Fauna transcends its bounds by movement from place to place.

And Man, how does he transcend his bounds? Man reaches outside of himself with words. With dialogue.

Man alone is capable of hearing his own self through the ears of another. Man alone is capable of transcending the very bounds of self.

174.

Make a part of your life an act that takes you beyond your bounds—helping people that are *not* part of your family or circle of friends, doing something that does *not* fit within your own self-definition.

Escape yourself.

175.

Have you ever heard of the "Saint in a Fur Coat"?

He sits in his house by a fireplace full of wood. But there is no fire. The house, and everyone in it are shivering from the cold. All except for him. He dons a fur coat and he is warm.

So we ask him, "Why do you warm only yourself? Why not kindle the wood in your fireplace and warm others as well?"

He answers, "It is not just this house. All the world is struck with a bitter, cold wind. Do you expect me to warm up an entire world?"

So we tell him that he does not have to warm up the entire world. But perhaps he could warm up one other individual. Perhaps two. Perhaps he could warm up one little *corner* of the world.

"For a person such as I," he replies, "it is not fitting to warm up only one corner."

And so there he sits, in his cold, dark house, all comfy in his fur coat.

176.

G-d told Noah that the world was to be destroyed. Noah asked what he should do.

G-d told him to build an ark to save his family and all the animal species. Noah built an ark.

After the flood, Noah beheld a desolate, empty world and broke into tears. "How, oh Merciful Creator," he plainted, "could you do such to your creation?!"

G-d replied, "Now you cry!? Now you have complaints!? You foolish shepherd! Where were your grievances when I first appeared to you? Had you spoken up then, you could have saved the world!"

Noah was a righteous man, but he was a Tzaddik in a fur coat.

177.

Abraham was a tzaddik of a different mold altogether.

G-d told Abraham He was about to destroy the cities of Sodom and Gemora—cities corrupt and evil to the core. Abraham argued, "Perhaps there are righteous people there! Will the Judge of All the Earth not do justice?"

Abraham felt a sense of ownership for the world in which he lived. If there was something wrong, it needed to be changed. Even if it had been decreed by the will of G-d.

178.

Moses took ownership of the dark as well as the light.
He argued not just for the righteous, but also for those
who had failed.

When the people angered G-d with a golden calf only
40 days after the revelation of Absolute Oneness at
Mount Sinai, Moses had to admit they had wronged.
Yet he did more than plead for them: He put his entire
being on the line for them.

"Forgive them!", He demanded. "And if you do not
forgive them, then wipe me out from Your book that
You have written!"

179.

The Rebbe wept profoundly as he spoke these words:

The entire being of Moses was the Torah he brought to
his people. The Torah was more than something he
taught. It was what he was. It was his G-d within him.

Yet when it came to a choice between the Torah or his
people, he chose his people. He said, "And if you do
not forgive them, then wipe me out from Your book
that You have written!"

His whole being was the Torah, but deep into his
essence, at the very core, was his oneness with his
people.

180.

Doing good is not about being nice.

You can do nice things all day long for many people, but it could be all just more service of your own self, food for your own ego.

He made a world where people would need each other, not so you could be nice, but to give you the opportunity to escape the confines of your own self.

This is why the Torah says, "If you see the donkey *of your enemy* crouching under its load, and your response is to abandon him there—then you must surely help him."

When you help those who show gratitude, when you lend a hand to those who are on your side, you are still within the realm of your own ego and self.

Help someone you don't want to help. Help him and learn to want to help him—only because this is the right thing to do.

At first, it may not feel so rewarding. But you have sprung free.

181.

We all have limitations—after all, are we not of flesh and blood? There comes a time, however, when you have to break out beyond those limits. You've got to do more than you can possibly do. The truth is, you not only have an animal soul, but a G-dly soul as well —and G-dliness knows no limits.

182.

There are people who believe they are doing good by swallowing other's egos alive. The egos of those they cannot help, and of those who cannot help them, are inedible to them—and therefore intolerable. They cannot work *with* others—because their egos leave no space for "others"—only for those extensions of their own inflated selves that show they *need* them, or whom *they* need.

You don't love your neighbor to glorify your own ego. When you come to your sister or brother's aid, leave your own self behind. Love with self-sacrifice.

183.

When you and the path you have chosen get along just great, it's hard to know whether your motives are sincere.

But when you come across a path to do good, and you see this path goes against every sinew of your flesh and every cell in your brain, when you want only to flee and hide from it— *do this*.

Then you shall know your motives are sincere.

184.

In truth, the world, standing on its own, is a place of exile and captivity.

Even when a man stands upright on the tallest mountain and perceives all there is to perceive, comprehends all that can be comprehended, achieves a realization of the Ultimate Oneness and Void that is behind all this—

But in the end, he is still stuck on the ground where his feet have brought him, his eyes have not seen beyond his own eyeballs, his mind has only comprehended that which he can know and reached that which is reachable—he has remained within his own self.

And the proof—he has remained with a G-d Who is above and an earth which is below, and the two cannot meet.

His only liberation, and the only liberation of the entire world, is when the One Above reaches down and tells us, "Do this. With this deed you are betrothed to Me."

And then there is no above and below. Then there is only One.

185.

Man, on his own, cannot reach higher than his own ego. He cannot break out of his own skin, he cannot lift himself up by pulling at his own hair. All of his achievements are tied to his own ego. All that he may comprehend is defined by his own subjective perception. He is a prisoner by virtue of existence.

So G-d threw Man a rope. He gave him tasks to fulfill that are beyond his comprehension, thoughts to fathom that take him outside the hollow of his subjective universe.

All that is needed is his willingness to leave himself.

We are all prisoners. But we sit on the keys.

186.

A glimmer of the soul descends to enclothe itself within your blood and flesh. The core of the soul remains above. Somehow, the two must be kept engaged.

Torah connects. When you throw your entire being into penetrating the depths of a word of Torah, meditating upon it until it penetrates to your bones—

Then a circuit has opened, connecting Above and Below to be as one.

...

Studying Torah and following its instructions takes Man beyond the bounds of a created being, into the limitless realm of the Creator.

187.

If you do His will only because it makes sense to you, then what has it got to do with Him? You are doing *your* will. You're back in prison.

188.

A person must be on fire—the fire of an altar burning up the ego inside, bringing the animal close to the divine.

A large ego burning makes a lot of noise.

A small ego burns quietly.

189.

Nothingness is the medium through which all energy moves, from above to below and from below to above.

Below, in Man, a sense of nothingness that transcends ego. Above, a Nothingness that transcends all boundaries and planes.

The nothingness below fuses with the Nothingness above, locking heaven and earth in eternal embrace.

That is why G-d is found amongst the truly humble.

190.

We are imprisoned because we have exiled our G-d.

As long as we search for G-d by abandoning the world He has made, we can never truly find Him.

As long as we believe there is a place to be escaped, there is no true liberation.

The ultimate liberation will be when we open our eyes to see that everything is here now.

It is there inside.

Everything is there inside.
But the "I" stands firmly guard at the gate.

TRUTH

In the beginning, people looked at the world about them in wonder. Then they began to make sense of whatever they could. But the wonder persisted. Eventually, they came to believe they could understand everything, that whatever does not make sense is simply not true—it does not exist. That's when the wonder died.

This is all a preamble to the Rebbe's approach to truth: Discard the notion that truth means that which make sense to you. Those who believed this were the ones who called Edison's light bulb a hoax while Menlo Park basked in it's light, who wrote theses to prove that man could not fly inside a machine when the Wright brothers had been doing just that publicly for five years. They are as foolish as the 18th century scientists who threw the meteorites out of the museums, because they said, "Rocks don't fall from the heavens, because there are no rocks in heaven!"

Truth is something you find by surrendering yourself to it. Truth is often something you would rather reject, something that refuses to sit inside your mind. Truth comes from somewhere beyond your grasp, beyond "you".

Once you have recognized that yes, this is the inescapable truth, then you must engage every cell of your brain to understand, to digest it. But begin with wonder, with emptiness, with open eyes and ears to what the world is telling you.

191.

To fool the world is one thing, but to fool yourself is
no big deal. You're a fool for wanting to fool yourself
—and anyone can fool a fool.

192.

People think that to attain truth you have to pulverize
boulders, move mountains and turn the world
upside-down. It's not so. Truth means talking to G-d
with sincerity, learning Torah knowing that this is
something G-dly, helping out the other guy
wholeheartedly—truth is found in the little things.

On the other hand, to move a mountain takes some
dynamite and a few bulldozers. To do one of those
little things can take a lifetime of working on yourself.

You do what you can: Learn and meditate and pray and
improve yourself in the ways you know how—and He
will help that what you do will be with Truth.

193.

There are many truths. There is a truth for every being
and for every particle of the universe—for each one
reflects its Master in a different way.

To seek truth means more than finding your own
truth. It means finding a truth that works for you and
for the other guy, for now and forever, in this place
and everywhere, for the body and for the soul, for the
sage and for the young, innocent child.

The higher the truth, the less boundaries it knows.

194.

The Baal Shem Tov taught that there are two paths:

1. G-dliness is everything.
2. Everything is G-dliness.

Where the two paths converge, there is G-d Himself.

195.

G-dliness is everything is the path of Abraham.
Abraham understood that there is a Reality beyond all
realities, before which no existence is true. Therefore
he smashed the idols and declared to all people and in
all places that there is only One.

Everything is G-dliness is the path of Isaac. Isaac saw
that the world is in truth G-dly. Therefore, Isaac dug
wells, in the earth and in the people. He dug away the
darkness and found the spark of G-dliness within each
thing.

Jacob struggled with the darkness.

196.

Each path contains what the other is missing: When G-dliness is everything, even the darkness is included. But the world is left untransformed, because there is no world—only G-dliness.

When everything is G-dliness, you transform the world by digging away the darkness to find the sparks of G-dliness. But the darkness remains piled up outside.

The path of Jacob is to find *That Which Is Everything* within each thing, and to bring *That Which Is Beyond All Things* to dwell within each thing. Jacob knows a G-d who is at once both beyond and within. To Jacob, darkness is also light.

197.

All that exists is Him
                    and you.

Everything else is just interface.

. . .

Everything that exists in your world is about
connecting to your Creator. Everything is one of three:

1. A connection to be grasped.

2. A disconnection to be avoided.

3. Or neutral ground. Awaiting you to transform it into
    a connection.

But if something was not part of your purpose, it
would not exist in your world.

198.

*How do
you
find the
center of
the surface
of a globe?*

In your world, all that exists is your Creator and you. In
the world of your neighbor, all that exists is his Creator
and him. And his world is just as true as yours.

In the world of a cow, there's just it's Creator and it. So
with an insect, so with a plant, so even with a rock.

Every seat of consciousness constitutes a world. And
each world is true.

*Each
individual
is the
center of
an entire
world.*

Knowing this is also part of your world: The knowledge
that in the other person's world you are only there as
an accessory, an interface by which he connects. And
now you know how to enter his world.

199.

The world is a place of constant change and unrest. Each point in time is distinct from the point before and the point after. Every point in space is its own entire world, with its own conditions and state of being. It is a world of fragments constantly rushing in a traffic of . seeming anarchy.

Look at your own life: You do so many different things, one after the other without any apparent connection between them.

Inner peace is when every part of you and every facet of your day is moving in the same direction. When you have purpose, you have peace.

200.

After 90 years soaked in Kaballa and philosophy ...

The ultimate prayer is the prayer of the small child.

·You pray to some lofty concept of The Infinite Light or The Essence of Being or...

But the child doesn't have any concept. Just G-d.

...

When you open your eyes in the morning, you are a new born child. Then and there you meet G-d face to face.

As you awaken and your brain becomes engaged, keep the child with you.

201.

The Light was concealed. But its Source was not. The Source of Light is everywhere.

202.

There is a G-d discovered by induction, a G-d of deduction, and there is something beyond all that.

You look at the world and see there is life within it. You have induced that there is a harmonious force within the creation.

You look at the world again and know that its Creator could have none of these constrictions—He must be an infinite G-d—and you have deduced a G-d entirely transcendent of all things you know.

But both these paths define G-d by the things you know—whether by finding Him within them, or by deducing that He is none of these and transcends them all. And that is as far as the mind can reach. It can reach upwards and upwards forever, but it can never grasp Him.

Deep inside, however, is a knowledge of a Being that is not defined, neither by what it is nor by what it is not.

As the Zohar says, "No thought can grasp Him. Yet He is grasped in the innermost stirrings of the heart."

203.

A sharp mind will find a truth for itself.

A humble spirit will find a truth higher than itself.

Truth is not the property of intellectuals, but of those who know how to escape their own selves.

204.

Many things are true in spirit, but the ultimate test of truth is here on earth.

205.

No man can claim to have reached the ultimate truth as long as there is another who has not.

Ultimate truth is an unlimited light—and if it is unlimited, how could it shine in one person's realm and not in another's?

206.

Rabbi Hillel of Paritch used to say, "I don't like fools, but someone not too smart for himself is closer to the truth."

207.

The essential teaching of the Baal Shem Tov:

Be simple, be earnest, and spread that simplicity throughout everything you do. Simplicity is a receptacle for G-d's simple Oneness.

HIGHER LIFE

Originally, this chapter was titled, "Afterlife". Then I came across a reply of the Rebbe to a college student who asked for an explanation of afterlife. The Rebbe replied that there is no such thing—life doesn't end, it just continues in a higher form.

208.

We don't say a person "will be going to heaven". We say this person is "a child of the world to come". Heaven is not just somewhere you go. It is something you carry with you.

209.

Rabbi Yochanan ben Zakkai, the Talmud relates, cried on his deathbed. When his disciples asked the reason for his tears, he replied, "I don't know on which path they will take me."

Apparently, until then, the matter hadn't crossed his mind.

Some people are constantly fretting over what will be with them in the end. Rabbi Yochanan was too busy thinking about what he had to do in the here and now. Up until the very last moment…

210.

Everything about the Rebbe was pure kindness. Even his idea of hell (in Hebrew: gehinom) was as kind and generous as could be:

People have a misconception of Hell. Let me tell you what Hell really is. Hell is a spiritual place where everything that exists in our world exists, but in an infinite way. So, whatever you chased after in this world, there you do it ad infinitum.

And that's Hell.

211.

Afterlife is a very rational, natural consequence of the order of things. After all, nothing is ever lost—even the body only transforms into earth. But nothing is lost.

The person you are is also never lost. It only returns to its source.

If your soul became attached to the material world during its stay here, then it must painfully rip itself away to make the journey back. But if it was only a traveller, connected to its source all along, then its ride home is heavenly.

212.

The Baal Shem Tov taught that in the heavenly court there is no one who can judge you for what you have done in your life on earth. So this is what they do:

They show you someone's life—all the achievements and all the failures, all the right decisions and all the wrongdoings—and then they ask you, "So what should we do with this somebody?"

And you give your verdict. Which they accept. And then they tell you that this somebody was you.

Of course, those who tend to judge others favorably have a decided advantage.

Better get in the habit now.

We Are All One

WE ARE ALL ONE

213.

I offer my hand of five fingers and you offer yours. Together we have a complete ten. This is a handshake: You and I are only fragments of the whole—until we come together.

214.

We are all fragments of greater souls, and those souls fragments of even more lofty ones, and so on with those—until we all link back to the one primordial soul: The soul of Adam.

None of us is complete. No one can stand on his or her own. What one is lacking the other fulfills, where one excels, another is wanting.

Only together can we find oneness in our own selves. Only together can we be a fit vessel for the One Above to be revealed.

215.

The Alter Rebbe wrote: The souls are all one. Only the bodies divide us.

. . .

The Alter Rebbe continued: Therefore, one who places the body before the spirit can never experience true love or friendship.

216.

In two ways, we are one: In our essence, and in our character.

In our essence, we are all one soul, with one source.

In our character, we are all complimentary of each other, none of us complete, each one contributing what the other lacks, each one adding his touch of perfection to his fellow. Like a massive jigsaw puzzle, we fit together to make a single perfect whole.

None of us is perfect without all the rest of us. And all the rest of us are incomplete when a single individual is missing.

217.

Once, I came home to find my children climbing into the attic through a hole in the ceiling—an act I had sternly forbidden due to the dangers involved. But I watched before I opened my mouth. It took four of them: Two to lift one up and another to hold the chair those two were standing on. It was then that I understood something I had heard my Rebbe say many times:

When a father sees his children working together with love, he is prepared to forgive them for anything. Better harmonious troublemaking than acrimonious obedience.

And so too with the Father Of Us All.

"Better they abandon me," He says, "than abandon one another."

218.

In his latter years, the Rebbe would stand for hours every Sunday, as thousands of people, both Jew and non-Jew would stand in line to receive his blessing. The Rebbe would look each person intently straight in the eyes for an eternal moment, often smiling, sometimes answering a question or providing advice, always giving his blessing or answering "amen" to the person's own request. Each person received from the Rebbe's hand a dollar bill to be given to any worthy cause of their choice.

All agreed that the spectacle was entirely supernatural. As the line went on, the Rebbe became more and more vitalized, as though he himself was receiving life from these people. When, after many hours, the line would finally come to an end, the Rebbe would turn to his personal secretary and ask, "Is there no one else?"

It happened that an elderly woman waited in line, sitting upon a small chair which she moved ahead together with the line. When she finally arrived before the Rebbe, she could no longer contain herself and burst out, "Rebbe, I am younger than you…and I only sat…and you stand here and greet each person… and just look at you!"

The Rebbe beamed and replied, "When you're counting jewels you don't get tired."

. . .

They asked the Alter Rebbe:, "Which is greater: Love of G-d, or love of your fellow man?"

He answered, "Love of your fellow man, for then you are loving that which your Beloved loves."

219.

Keep your trust in G-d to yourself. When things don't go so well, tell yourself it is all really for the good, and rejoice in however G-d treats you.

But when others come with their troubles, telling them they should rejoice in their afflictions is plain callousness. Cry for them, pray for them, do everything you can for them—and *then* you can tell them to trust in G-d.

...

A young artist who had suffered several years of depression and inner strife came to the Rebbe and told his story. The Rebbe listened, every minute or so wiping the beads of perspiration from his forehead.

220.

Do not be dismayed by the hypocrisy of others, nor by
your own inconsistencies. Our lives are all journeys
through hills and valleys—no man's spiritual standing
is a static affair.

But the good each person achieves is eternal, as he
connects to the Source of All Good, Who is infinite and
everlasting. The failures, on the other hand, are
transient and superficial, fleeting shadows of clouds, as
stains in a garment to be washed away.

221.

Rabbi Akiva taught to love your fellow man to the point
of giving your life for him. Yet his students died of a
plague because they did not treat each other with
respect. How could it be?

There are times when love can kill. There are times
when you love someone so much, you cannot allow
him to breath. He must do things the way *you*
understand is best for him—because you cannot bear
that one you love so much should be in any way
distant from the truth as you know it.

"After all," you imagine, "I must do for him what I
would have done for myself!"

But true love makes room for the one you love.

As Hillel the Elder put it, "That which is hateful to you,
do not do to your fellow."

True love is best expressed not in what you do and
what you say, but in what you *do not* do, and what you
do not say.

222.

One who is full of himself fills all the space around him. There is no room left for anyone else. Therefore, he despises another person by virtue of the space that other person consumes. He may give reasons for his disdain, but the reasons are secondary.

This is called *wanton hatred*. It is the reason given for our exile. It is the core of all evil. It is balanced and cured by wanton acts of love and kindness.

223.

Someone wrote that he had, in his administrative duties, taken an action that fiercely angered one of his associates and turned him against him.

The Rebbe replied:

Bring into your heart a deep love of this man, and his anger will spontaneously disappear.

224.

Once a distinguished rabbi complained to the Tzemach Tzedek (the third rebbe of Lubavitch) that nobody cared for his opinion and that his colleagues stepped all over him.

The Tzemach Tzedek replied, "Who told you to spread yourself around so much that wherever anybody steps they must step on you?"

225.

The Tzemach Tzedek once told someone to become an onion.

This was a person who had been travelling from town to town spreading Chassidic teachings. But now he had stopped. All the fuss over himself and his talents, he claimed, had been feeding his ego. Now he had to work with himself to diminish that negative aspect of his character.

The Tzemach Tzedek showed no pity. "An onion should become of you!" he cried, "But teach others what you must teach them!"

...

Why an onion? An onion is thrown in the pot not so that we may eat onion, but only to give flavor to the chicken and the broth. Like the onion, you sometimes need to sacrifice your own personal growth so others may grow.

And that is growth.

226.

The first stages of your life are to learn to be a master over yourself. But then comes a major and difficult transition in life, when you take on the responsibilities of a family. Now you must learn to put aside your own self improvement for their sake.

But you surely realize that, in the long run, what is best for them will be best for you.

227.

To someone who wrote he was avoiding social activism because it had been feeding his ego:

"And without the activism there is no ego? Better a haughty activist than a self-centered do-nothing!"

228.

People misunderstand the meaning of tolerance.

Tolerance doesn't mean seeing someone harming himself and saying, "Live and let live". That's indifference. Apathy. If you see someone going the wrong way and you care about him, you'll do everything you can to set him straight.

Tolerance means that although you see his faults in all their ugliness naked before you, that doesn't decrease by one iota your respect for him as a fellow human being, and for all the good he has within him.

And if you say, "How can I be expected to lead a life of paradox, to both respect and rebuke at once?"

Let me ask you, do *you* have any faults? And do you not respect yourself nonetheless?

If you can live a life of paradox for yourself, you can give at least that privilege to the other guy.

229.

Until you can see the good within a person you are incapable of helping him.

230.

If you rebuke your brother and he does not listen,
then it is you who is to blame. Words from the heart
enter the heart.

231.

Talk is powerful. Speak bad about someone and you
expose all the ugliness in him, in yourself and in
whoever happens to be paying attention. Once
exposed, the wound begins to fester and all are hurt.

Speak good about the same person, and the inner
good within him, within you and within all who
participate begins to shine.

232.

We have a tradition from the Baal Shem Tov that when
someone tells you "not good things" about another
person, you should feel great pain and distress.

Because, either way you look at it, someone is hurting:
If the story about this person is true, then things are
not good for him. And if the report is false, then the
one who has fabricated it is hurting.

233.

The very fact you know about someone who is in
trouble means that in some way you are able to help.
Otherwise, why would this knowledge have entered
your world?

. . .

Arik Sharon, when he was Israeli Minister of Defence, came to visit the Rebbe. After his private audience, he related to his friends, "The Rebbe was very cordial. He asked when I was leaving, and when I told him I was taking a flight back tomorrow he insisted that I stay a little longer."

General Sharon's Lubavitcher friends explained to him that the Rebbe doesn't say such things just out of politeness and insisted that he postpone his flight.

The plane that Sharon was to have taken was hijacked to Libya.

At a later date, another Israeli cabinet member, in private audience with the Rebbe, poised the obvious question. "If you knew," he asked the Rebbe, "why did you not report the matter to the authorities and attempt to circumvent the whole hijacking?"

"Do you think I knew?" the Rebbe responded in a very serious tone.

"It is not a matter of prophecy or knowing. It is simply that when I see someone standing before me, I am so completely obsessed with doing that person a favor—that is why I say what I say."

234.

Every person you meet has a wellspring deep inside, If you can't find it, the fault is yours. Remove the rust from your shovel, sharpen its blade, and dig harder and deeper.

235.

Our souls cannot be broken that they should need repair, nor deficient that they should need anything added. Our souls need only to be uncovered and allowed to shine.

236.

People are mirrors for each other. If you see the faults of another person and they don't leave you alone, it is truly your own faults you see.

This is G-d's great kindness to us, for without this device we would never be able to determine our true faults.

237.

One of the most unforgettable talks I ever heard from the Rebbe was the time he spoke to the handicapped Israeli soldiers. Make that, "the special Israeli soldiers".

Each and every person is given all he needs to accomplish his mission in this world. But each of us have different missions, and therefore need different powers to accomplish them. Yet none of us has an easier time than any other.

Therefore, if you see a human being who appears deficient or "handicapped", know that in truth that person must have compensatory powers others do not have. Do not call him "handicapped"—call him "special".

...

An Israeli soldier lost his two legs when a Syrian land mine exploded beneath his jeep.

His mother came to him in the hospital and cried.

His father sat silent.

Generals and leaders came and made their speeches to him proclaiming him a hero and one to be proud of.

There was no condolence. The people still avoided him in the street.

The Rebbe shook his hand, looked him straight in the eye and said, "Thank you."

The "thank you" is still carrying him.

238.

To a rabbi and talmudic scholar who asked the Rebbe for a blessing for peace of mind so that he could devote himself to his studies:

Peace of mind! Peace of mind! The world is burning! Children go on the streets ignorant of all you have to teach them! And all you can think of is your own peace of mind?!!

We Are All One

ACTS OF
BEAUTY

When I was a kid, radical political activism was cool. By age fourteen, I was heavily involved.

But no matter how much you did, there was always this classic dilemma of "Hey, I'm only one out of six billion! And so is the guy next to me. It just does not seem plausible we could really make a difference!"

It didn't matter that you saw with your own eyes how much could be accomplished, that you had case after case history to demonstrate how one person could turn around an entire world. It's a matter of cognitive dissonance—something the human mind simply cannot accept until some explanation is given.

The Rebbe gave an explanation: My problem was that I was only looking at the physical, observable world, but not what's behind it—somewhat analogous to seeing the control panel and not the engine. Sure, the deed is something that happens in the concrete, mundane world, but where there is a heart and soul behind the deed, then there is an effect deep within the metaphysical bowels of the natural order. So, just as one small button can trigger global reaction, one small deed can generate earth-shaking results.

239.

Never underestimate the power of a simple, pure deed done from the heart.

The world is not changed by men who move mountains, nor by those who lead the revolutions, nor by those whose purse strings tie up the world.

Dictators are deposed, oppression is dissolved, entire nations are transformed by a few precious acts of beauty performed by a handful of unknown soldiers.

In fact, it was Maimonides who wrote in his code of law, "Each person must see himself as though the entire world were held in balance and any deed he might do could tip the scales."

240.

Rabbi Judah the Prince said, "Know that which is above you."

The Maggid of Mezritch explained, "Know that everything that occurs above comes from you."

All that came into being...

...all the created worlds and all the ethereal entities that live in them, even the worlds that are mere emanations without tangible substance, even the worlds of thought and beyond to the realms of infinite light that preceded Creation...

—all this came to be only as a result of the thought of you, the earthly being, struggling in a world that only a infinitesimal glimmer of G-dliness has reached in its purity, bringing light where light could not be.

And so it follows, that with one simple act of beauty, all those worlds and angels and realms of light become liberated and elevated and reciprocate with a burst of illumination into our lowly world.

That is why the entire creation can be transformed with one simple, sincere deed. Never underestimate the power of light.

241.

When you reach the final ascent of the climb, you cling to whatever twig or feeble root you can find to pull yourself up.

And that is where we are now. Any spark of light that comes your way—squeeze all you can from it.

242.

As soon as you start measuring good deeds, to determine which is greater, which takes priority over the other—you have already entered precarious ground.

Your job is to do whatever is sent your way.

243.

Some people think that if they did something beautiful yesterday, or last week, or even several years ago, they've done their part and G-d should continue paying them for it the rest of their life. It's something like loaning money—you lend it to someone last year and you're still making a profit off him today.

Problem is, the Torah prohibits charging interest —even from G-d.

If you did good yesterday, do twice as good today.

244.

Do not give charity.

Giving charity means being nice and giving away your
money. But who says it is your money to begin with? It
is money put in your trust, to be disbursed for good
things and for others when they will need it.

Change your attitude. Instead of doing what is nice, do
what is *right*. Put the money where it belongs.
This we call צדקה—tzedaka .

...

Do not pray.

Prayer means there are two entities, one entity
petitioning a higher one.

Instead of praying, connect. Become one with your
Maker, so that divine energy will come through you
and into our world to heal the sick ,to cause the rain to
fall...
This we call תפילה —*tefilla.*

...

Do not repent.

Repentance means to stop being bad and to become
good.

But your essential being is always good. The bad is only
on the outside. So instead of repenting , return. Return
to the essential self and to what is rightfully yours.
This we call תשובה—t'shuva.

245.

Our view of the world and its Creator's view are very different.

From our perspective, there is always a giver and a taker. Whether the merchandise be knowledge, affection, or money—somebody always seems to come out on top and someone else on the bottom.

But why are there those who have and those who have not? Certainly, this is part of the Creator's plan, so there could be kindness and giving in His world.

Which means that in the Creator's view, giver and taker are one. The taker is really giving and the giver receiving, for without this whole process the giver would be forever imprisoned within his own self. There is no higher and lower.

246.

There is compassion that feeds the ego and there is compassion that humbles it.

Compassion that feeds the ego is a sense of pity for those who stand beneath you.

Compassion that humbles is born of a deeper understanding of the order of things: When you understand that your fellow man is suffering in order that you may be privileged to help him—then you are truly humbled.

247.

Sometimes it happens that you set out to do something with the best of intentions—and you end up with what appears the opposite.

Know with absolute certainty—because this is a tradition of our sages—that if your true intent is good, then only good can come out of it. Perhaps not the good you intended—or care for—but good nevertheless.

248.

The Rebbe's most common response to someone who had done something positive:

It is the nature of Man that he never attains half his goal. When he hits the 100 mark, he must make 200. And when he attains 200, he demands of himself 400.

So, too, must you always be growing in your acts of kindness.

...

When the mayor of Haifa came to the Rebbe for his blessings, the Rebbe blessed him with the powers of the Infinite. To which the mayor replied that he is satisfied with whatever he can get. The Rebbe responded, exasperated:

"And what do the inhabitants of Haifa gain from you being satisfied with whatever you can get?"

249.

Giving affects not only the one you give to, but also you, the giver. Therefore, it's not only important how much you give, but how often. Each act of giving uplifts and purifies you a little more.

Keep a small charity box attached to the wall in a conspicuous place, and place a few coins in it every day. Keep one in your home and one in your office.

250.

When you give for a worthy cause, it is really only a loan and G-d Himself is the guarantor. Furthermore, the more you give, the more you get.

I don't mean this figuratively. I say so you will test it and see for yourself.

251.

Perhaps the Rebbe's most common words: The main thing is: do something!

BETWEEN WOMAN AND MAN

Now is my chance for a note on gender usage:

I use "...him" and "he will....", "a man" and all the other non-PC terms. The fact is, the Rebbe generally used the neutral Yiddish form of "one" as in "one will...". In Hebrew, the Rebbe was careful to use both the masculine and feminine form of "one will". English is terribly clumsy with these things, so I've committed the sins of mistranslation you read here.

252.

There were always special, unique women who studied and taught Torah. But today, many women are learning Torah and affecting the world in a way as never before.

In the times of Moshiach, the superior quality of women will be revealed. What we see now is a glimmer and a preparation for those times.

253.

Of the very great tzaddikim, many had wives greater than themselves and daughters greater than their sons. So it was with Abraham, Isaac and Jacob. So it was with Rabbi Akiva and Rabbi Meir. So it was with many great masters of Chassidism.

This is because these tzaddikim, in their personal lives, were already tasting of the World to Come.

254.

When you look carefully into the story of the exodus, you see that the true redeeming force was the faith of the women. Today, history is repeating itself.

255.

When G-d made the world He gave each creature, each nation and each individual a role and a meaning. When each plays its part there is harmony. When the lines become too blurred, there is acrimony.

256.

A metaphor of the Talmud: A man works in the field and brings home wheat—but shall he then eat wheat? Of what use is his toil?

His wife grinds the wheat into flour and makes bread.

So too, the tasks of life: A man's spiritual accomplishments only become realized in the material world due to his wife.

257.

Changing the world is a twofold task.

Bringing spirituality into the world is principally the man's task. Elevating the world to become spiritual is principally the woman's task.

Men, generally, are meant to deal with the present. The future—and those who will live within it—is in the hands of the women.

258.

From your father you may learn the things you must do. From your mother you learn who you are.

That is why Jewish identity follows a matriarchal lineage.

259.

The most central aspects of life, G-d handed over to the woman.

...

Women have a greater obligation to study the esoteric side of Torah than men.

260.

You write that you and your spouse always seem to disagree on every issue. But this is the natural way we were created. We all have our own minds. It's alright to disagree. Now you must learn to give in.

261.

You complain that peace in the home is, for you, wrought with obstacles.

All of us today are souls that have been here before. In general, we return on unfinished business. Certainly, we are all responsible for doing all the good we can, and avoiding everything harmful. But that certain unfinished business, that is where the most obstacles shall be.

And those obstacles will be your only clue as to what business you are here to finish.

262.

The relation of husband and wife is the way our world reflects the relationship of the Creator with His Creation. There is nothing more pivotal to the world's ultimate fulfillment than this.

Therefore, as the world nears closer and closer to its fulfillment, the resistance grows stronger and stronger. By now, absolutely everything appears to be undermining the most crucial key of peace between man and woman.

263.

Marriage is a microcosm of the soul's descent into this world:

If you are here looking for what you can get out of this world, then the world and all its trappings will only drag you down.

But if you are looking for what you can give, then you, your part of the world, and your soul all are uplifted and filled with light.

So too, when you enter a marriage: Look for what you can give, and reap harmony and love.

264.

The best strategy for reducing quarrels is that proposed by wise King Solomon, "A gentle reply defuses wrath."

When you can give in, give in. And on those matters that you cannot concede—avoid making a major issue out of them. Be pliant in the wind like a reed, and not hard and brittle like a cedar.

When your spouse will see you are not interested in making battle, but return bullets with flowers, cannon fire with sweetness, slowly, slowly the warfare will let up and you'll be able to sit and amicably work out the real issues.

265.

Even if all your complaints about your spouse are well founded and valid—show her your love, nevertheless. Show her unconditional love.

It is said that all our exile is due to the sin of unmitigated hatred. When each one of us will start with unmitigated love in our own domain, from there it will spread to all else that we do, and from there to the entire world, speedily in our days, amen.

266.

Woman have a greater sensitivity to emotional issues than men. So when there is a quarrel, generally it is the man's job to concede to his wife.

267.

A good wife is one who makes her husband want the right things.

268.

The blessings a man receives, according to our sages, are not for himself, but for his wife and on her account. And so, they said, "Honor your wife so you may become wealthy."

269.

Nothing is greater than peace. Even when you are 100% right, and you know your spouse is 100% wrong, you can still give in for the sake of peace.

...

Better a difficult peace than an easy quarrel.

CHILDREN

The Rebbe, sadly, never had any children. Yet they were so important to him. Whenever he would pass by a child he would reach in his pocket and pull out a dime—for the child to put in a charity box. Certainly there are few men of his stature who spent as much time addressing gatherings of children, speaking, writing and publishing works aimed at the children.

To the Rebbe, children were important not just for what they would become, but for what they are in the present tense. He ascribed to their prayers and their good deeds tremendous power, much more than the power of adults.

The child he saw as a lucid, glistening crystal vessel in which to find G-d. More than once the Rebbe pointed out how his own thoughts strove to attain the simplicity of those of a child. In that simplicity, he taught, can be found the simplicity of the Infinite.

Lubavitch publishes a children's magazine called "Moshiach Times". The Rebbe expressed to the editor several of his concerns: That the publication should reach to the youngest children; that real people—not strange-looking animals—should be used as role models; and that there be a parity of pictures of girls and pictures of boys.

270.

If you want to see the face of the Moshiach, just look at the children!

271.

G-d delights when little children jump and play on His holy books. Not that we should encourage it…but at least we can provide the holy books.

272.

Give a child kind, non-predatory stuffed animals to play with, like sheep, deer, giraffe and such. What the child looks at in those delicate years has a permanent affect.

And earlier still: Life starts in the womb. Sing to the fetus good things and let it hear words of Torah.

273.

Sometimes you don't know whether to punish a child or hug him. If you punish him when he needed a hug, you've made a serious mistake. But if you hug him when he should have been punished, so you've got an extra mitzvah.

274.

A married couple asked for a blessing that their children behave properly. The Rebbe's reply seems simple, but since I have not seen it in any parenting book I'm including it here. Sometimes the most obvious is also the most inconvenient —and therefore the most avoided:

Behave properly yourselves. When the children see your example, they will naturally want to do the same as their parents. Then it is only a matter of talking with them, step by step, day after day, and eventually it will help.

275.

When Moshiach comes, the teachers of small children will be in the first row to greet him.

...

The Rebbe formed a club for Jewish children called "Tzivos Hashem". He told the children that with verses of Torah and good deeds they would fight the forces of darkness in the world and bring Moshiach.

The children began to stand close to the Rebbe at public gatherings. Some went under the table near his feet. Legend has it that occasionally a small hand would rise up from under the table to snatch a piece of the Rebbe's cake.

Finally, one of the adults became fed up with this lack of decorum and attempted to escort some children away.

The Rebbe turned to him and exclaimed, "You are only a civilian and they are soldiers—and *you* want to remove *them?*"

276.

Until recently, it was always considered the greatest of blessings to have many children.

Wealth is not a mansion filled with silver and gold. Wealth is children and grandchildren growing up on the right path.

277.

Every day, take one half hour to think about your children and where they're headed. Then do all you can about it. Then do more.

ALL NOAH'S CHILDREN

278.

On the failure of Marxism:

The most ingenious socio-political system of the most brilliant men is doomed to failure. Our minds are bribed and able to justify anything. Our laws are always relative and challengeable.

see the appendix

For mankind to exist in harmony, we must listen to the voice that Noah heard after the flood. We must accept that there is a set of absolute values set by the Creator of the world, values that cannot be played about with to suit our convenience. Values from beyond the subjective minds of men.

279.

post-humanism

People call me "old-fashioned" for my belief in an ancient and timeless teaching and for my faith in G-d. In truth, it is they who are old-fashioned, for they cling to an idea that failed decades ago.

The Age of Reason, of Enlightenment, of Humanism—when Knowledge and Intellect were worshipped as the Redeemers of Mankind—all this died and was buried when the most civilized and intellectual nation on earth committed the most unthinkable atrocities.

Man, *to survive*, must accept, feel, stand in awe and connect to That Which Is Above Him.

280.

If you tell a child, "Keep this rule because if you don't you will be punished!" the child has two doubts in his mind: Maybe he won't be caught, and if he is caught, maybe the punishment won't outweigh the crime.

The child has to know that there is an eye that sees, an ear that hears—that there is a Higher Unseen Being to which he is answerable. This is the only way to reduce crime in America.

...

In our zeal to separate church and state, we have effectively removed any concept of the supernal or the spiritual from the classroom. A child grows up today learning about a face-value world centered around his own self. There is no awe.

281.

I was there in Germany before the war, and I tell you, the same thing could happen here in America if the subject of morality is not allowed to enter the public schools.

282.

In the early sixties the Rebbe repeated many times:

There will come a time when not only will Russia *allow* the Jews to leave, but they will *assist* with their emigration to the Holy Land. Then we shall know that the redemption is imminent.

283.

At the time of the disarmament talks in the U.N. (January 1992):

When the Prophet Isaiah said, "They shall beat their swords into plough shares," he was referring to the end of the Cold War and the beginning of nuclear disarmament. The prophecy has only begun to be realized.

...

The Cold War did not end due to Man's power of reason. War never made sense—yet the same rational Man has fought them for millennium. All that is new is that the light of Moshiach has begun to shine in our world.

THE BLUEPRINT
OF CREATION

The Rebbe's principal activity was studying —pouring over the texts of the Talmud, the legal codes and responsum, Kaballa and philosophy—every aspect of the wealth of Torah, examining and comparing from every angle, asking the questions others were afraid to ask and providing solutions nobody thought to answer.

True, he was running an international activist organization with hundreds of offices across the globe. True, he received bags of mail every day. True, he himself was the one who demanded action and not just ideas. Yet his principal occupation—what he spoke about, what he wrote about, how he spent most of the hours of his day—was Torah study.

The Rebbe often repeated that through the study of Torah you could conquer the world. And from the way the Rebbe discussed Torah you could see he was doing just that: Every thought, every teaching was a new understanding of the entire universe. A simple story or a seemingly dry legalistic point became in his hands an insight to the workings of time and space.

In fact, spending that degree of time on study is a strong statement in itself. It says, "This of me that you see involved in the world and its affairs, this is not me

—this is a mere glimmer of my soul. Where I truly am is in an intimate union with a G-dly teaching that is beyond time and beyond the whole creation."

Only one who is firmly anchored in a higher realm can effect true change within our world.

284.

They translate it as "The Bible", or "The Law", but that's not what the word means. Torah means "instructions". Whatever piece of Torah you learn, you *must* find the instructions it is giving you.

285.

Torah is the blueprint by which the world was designed. Everything that exists can be found in the Torah. Even more: In any one concept of Torah you can find the entire world.

286.

When G-d spoke to Man at Mount Sinai, tradition tells there was no echo.

Torah penetrates and is absorbed by all things, because it is their essence. There is no place where it does not apply, no darkness it does not illuminate, nothing it cannot bring alive. Nothing will bounce it back and say, "Torah is too holy to belong here."

287.

Before the experience at Mount Sinai, there was a hierarchy of truth. The high priest of Egypt had the real truth. The scribes had secrets of the truth. Their initiated students had inklings. The people wallowed in ignorance.

At Sinai, all men, women and children had to be present. All received the same truth, all at once.

When it comes to the genuine article, there is no higher and lower. Some may perceive a truth in greater depth or in broader detail, but the essence of truth is equally everywhere and for everybody. Because G-d is everywhere.

288.

Go out on a clear night and see the moon reflected in the water of a lake. Then see the very same moon reflected in a pond, in a teacup, in a single drop of water. So the same essential Torah is reflected within each person who studies it, from a small child to a great sage.

289.

Before the experience at Mount Sinai, there was earth
and there was heaven. If you wanted one, you were
obliged to abandon the other.

At Mount Sinai, the boundaries of heaven and earth
were broken and Man was empowered to fuse the two:
To raise the earthly into the realm of the spirit, and to
bring heaven down to earth.

...

Before the experience of Mount Sinai, the coarse
material of which the world is made could not be
elevated. It could be used as a medium, an aid in
achieving enlightenment, but it itself could not
be enlightened.

Jacob used sticks for meditation. Isaac dug wells.
But neither the sticks nor the wells became imbued
with G-dliness.

All that changed at Mount Sinai. When you take a piece
of leather and write upon it a Torah scroll, you have
transformed the material into spiritual. And the same
with flour used for matzah for Passover night, and
branches used to cover a succah, and even the
earnings which you tithe for good causes. And so you
may do in every aspect of your life.

Our forefathers task was to enlighten the souls of men.
Ours is to transform the material darkness into light.

290.

People think the Torah is all about laws and customs
and quaint stories, with a mystical side as well.

The experience of our people at Mount Sinai was a
mystical one. The biblical account says they *saw* the
thunder. They saw that which is normally heard, and
they heard that which is normally seen. The spiritual
became their reality, and the earthly became an
ethereal inference, an intellectual fancy.

The soul of the Torah—its mystical experience
—came first. Torah without its inner meaning is a
body without a soul.

291.

There are not two Torahs, one for mystics and one for
legalists. There is the body of Torah and there is the
soul of Torah. It is all one. Neither can contradict the
other, and in each the other can be found.

292.

In a simple commentary written for a five year old,
great secrets of the Torah can be found. But only once
you understand the simple commentary as the five
year old does.

293.

To involve your entire self you must be creative in
Torah. To be creative in Torah you must lock out
the self.

294.

Sometimes the Torah will tell you one thing, later contradict itself, and then later reveal a third concept that settles the contradiction.

With Torah, you don't get all the answers at once. First you must absorb and live with one simple truth. Then later you must find another truth—one that may seem to conflict with and negate all you previously learned. Then, from that confusion, emerges a higher truth—the inner light behind all you had learned before.

295.

Rabbi Zera fasted 100 fasts to forget all he had learned in Babylonia, so he could go on to learn the Torah of the Land of Israel.

Learning is not the mere acquisition of knowledge and more knowledge. Learning is a process of making quantum leaps beyond the subjective self. No matter how high a summit you may reach, there is always another peak above.

But you can only reach that peak once you realize you are still in the valley.

296.

You may ask, "Why must I study and learn? Is not the truth already within me?"

The truth is locked within you, deep in slumber. It is awakened and liberated by the truth that comes from without.

297.

Studying Torah is not like studying any other subject.
In another subject your mind fuses itself with
information and knowledge *about* a thing. But in
learning Torah, those thoughts you contemplate —He
is there within them and you are one with Him at that
time.

298.

When you hear a concept of Torah, you must meditate
upon it. You must take what you hear from a state of
understanding to a state of realization and vision. It
must move you until you are no longer the same self
and your day is no longer the same day. Then it has
become yours.

299.

You can live in a palace filled with treasures and still be
poor. To be wealthy you must *own* the things you
have.

So too with poverty of the mind: You may have all the
knowledge and brilliant ideas in the world, but you are
still poor until they have become part of you.

300.

The order of your day is crucial. It must start with vision and only then gradually immerse into the world.

Begin with learning that inspires, with meditation and prayer. Then go on to study of Torah that deals with worldly matters.

And then you may plunge ahead into the darkness, full of light with which to illuminate it.

301.

A student begins as a sponge or as a funnel: Either everything is absorbed, undiscerningly—or everything passes in one ear and out the other. The first job of a teacher, therefore, is to direct the student and tell him, "Focus on this, this is important. Do not focus on this— this is only the background."

302.

I don't believe in philosophy. I believe in ideas that change people.

...

The Rebbe initiated a campaign to turn Jewish people back to traditional Jewish practice. The entire campaign was focussed on getting people to do things, such as lighting a candle on Friday before sunset, putting a few pennies in a charity box every day, wearing tefillin every morning, etc.. The Rebbe emphasized again and again: Don't get into debate, don't get lost in philosophy. Just get people to do, and talk about it later.

Many criticized the campaign for this emphasis on action. "People need to understand what they are doing, or else it is empty ritual," they argued.

The Rebbe replied:

People are not changed by arguments, nor by philosophy. People are changed by *doing*. Introduce a new habit into your life, and your entire perspective of the world changes.

First *do*, then learn about what you are already doing.

303.

Every created being is both the sun and the moon.

The sun gives constantly of its warmth and its light. The moon, on the other hand, only reflects the light it receives from the sun.

So too, there is nothing in G-d's world that may only take without giving. And there is nothing that may give without receiving. Every created being must both give and receive, be the sun as well as the moon.

304.

Every created being is both the sun and the moon.

The sun is constant—every day the same fiery ball rises in the sky. But the moon cycles through constant change—one day it is whole, then it wanes until it has disappeared all together. Yet, then it is renewed, returning from nothingness.

So too, every created being must both grow and change like the moon—and yet stay ever constant as the sun.

Grow, change and constantly learn—yet always stand firm, knowing who you are.

305.

A container is defined by its contents: A pitcher of water is water. A crate of apples is apples. A house, too, is defined by what it contains.

Fill your house with books of Torah, and your house becomes a Torah. Affix charity boxes to its walls, and your house becomes a wellspring of charity. Bring those who need a warm home to your table, and your house becomes a lamp in the darkness.

306.

If you're serious about something, it has a fixed time. If you're earnest about getting something done and the phone rings, you ignore it.

The spiritual side of your life is not a hobby nor a luxury—it is your purpose of existence. When you are learning Torah, or meditating or in prayer, nothing else exists.

Your spiritual career should have *at least* equal priority to your worldly career.

FAITH &
INTELLECT

They say someone asked the Rebbe's wife what she thought of her husband. "I'll tell you one thing," she replied. "My husband believes in G-d."

She wasn't joking. After the holocaust, G-d's stocks had never been lower. Even the staunchest believer was conflicted. And from that dust and smoldering ashes a new generation had to be raised.

(In truth, I don't know who had the greater struggle: Those who were brought up with faith and then witnessed the holocaust, or whose who were brought up on the holocaust, on cynicism and materialism and then struggled with faith—meaning my own generation.)

Yet, through his letters, his talks, his actions and just by being who he was, the Rebbe, more than anyone else, restored faith to the Jews.

Great faith of a simple mind is not so impressive. Simple faith of a great mind is. Perhaps the simple person just hasn't asked the right questions. Perhaps faith is convenient for him. Perhaps he's afraid of what his wife might do to him if he came home one day and announced he no longer believes.

A truly great mind is not swayed by such concerns. Nothing forces him to believe—he believes because it is the truth. And since his faith is not self-serving, but founded on a truth beyond the self, therefore it is absolute, it is unshakable, down to the detail. And very infectious.

307.

From a letter:

You write to me you are concerned that you don't believe. If you don't believe, then why does not believing concern you?

From another letter:

I do not accept your assertion that you do not believe. For if you truly had no concept of a Supernal Being Who created the world with purpose, then what is all this outrage of yours against the injustice of life? The substance of the universe is not moral, and neither are the plants and animals. Why should it surprise you that whoever is bigger and more powerful swallows his fellow alive?

It is only due to an inner conviction in our hearts, shared by every human being, that there is a Judge, that there is right and there is wrong. And so, when we see a wrong, we demand an explanation: Why is this not the way it is supposed to be?

That itself is belief in G-d.

308.

There is sub-rational faith— faith in dogma. Then there is super-rational faith—intuitive knowledge, consciousness of a higher reality, a glimmer of the infinite within the finite human being.

Our job is not to *have* faith. We have faith already, whether we want it or not. It comes in our blood from our ancestors who gave their lives for it. Our job is to transport that higher vision that gave them their faith down into our minds, into our personalities, into our words, into our actions in daily life. To make it part of our selves and our world.

309.

Intellect is crippled in its approach to the Divine —after all, logic, the criteria of what makes sense and what doesn't, is itself no more than a creation, a whim of a Supreme Creator who is infinitely beyond intellect.

To approach the One Who Created Intellect, requires a sense which is beyond intellect. We call this sense אמונה— *emuna*, which some translate as faith.

310.

That there are matters we don't understand is obvious—how could the finite intellect of an inherently subjective mortal being, imprisoned within the confines of time and space, be expected to fathom the infinite wisdom of the Creator?

The great wonder is that there are matters we *can* understand.

311.

Any reason we may suppose for G-d's will could not be
the ultimate reason. The finite mind cannot begin to
fathom an infinite wisdom—never mind that which
brought forth wisdom from the Void.

The ultimate knowledge is that we do not know.

312.

True, G-d knows all before it occurs. More than that: It
is His knowledge that brings all events into being.

But we still have free choice.

You claim this is illogical. I ask you: Knowledge of
existence before any thought of any thing exists
_is_ logical?

When we talk about the Source of All Existence, our
principles of logic no longer apply. We don't
understand a thing, because there is no understanding.

313.

If I could understand, if I could observe and conclude
all this empirically, I would not need faith. The power
of faith is that it reaches beyond the bounds of our
finite minds.

...

If G-d were only a little smarter than me, He wouldn't
be my G-d.

314.

Don't imagine that you can escape faith. Every science, every system of logic, has its axioms. Reason cannot move one step forward without some assumption upon which to base itself.

315.

Let's say you saw a magnificent machine, with hundreds of thousands of parts, all working in spectacular unison and harmony, far beyond anything the human mind could contrive. And you examined the details of this machine and found that some aspects of its workings puzzle you. Would you complain to the inventor? Or would you pray in awe for understanding?

Yet, to G-d you have complaints!

316.

This was an emotional experience. The Rebbe spoke about the suffering in the world, and when he came to these words began to choke and sob:

If He is truly capable of anything, then why can't He provide good without the bad? And if His Torah contains the answers for all questions, why does it not answer this one?

There could be only one answer: He does not wish us to know, because if we knew we would become complacent.

317.

Abraham, father of us all, questioned G-d's justice. So did Moses. So did Akiva. So did many enlightened souls. You are not the first.

Of all those who questioned, there were two approaches: Those who meant it, and those who did not.

Those who wanted understanding gained understanding—a sense of nothingness encountering a reality far beyond our puny minds.

Those who asked but did not want to understand gained nothing.

. . .

Elie Wiesel asked the Rebbe, "How can you believe in G-d after the holocaust?"

The Rebbe asked Elie Wiesel, "How can you not believe in G-d after the holocaust?"

Last I heard, Elie Wiesel was believing in G-d.

318.

You ask me, "Why did G-d allow it to happen?"

You recognize that everything in this world has purpose and meaning. Examine any aspect of His vast Creation, from the cosmos to the workings of the atom and you will see there *must* be a plan.

And so you ask, where does *this* fit into the plan? *How* could it?

I can only answer, painfully, G-d alone knows.

But what I cannot know, I need not know.

I need not know in order to fulfill that which my Creator has created me to do.

And that is, to change the world so this could never happen again.

319.

If your belief system is based upon what makes sense to you, what you find most gratifying and what best accommodates your own self concept—then you will undoubtedly fear intellectual inquiry. At best, your approach will be subjective and bribed.

However, when your faith is based not upon your subjective self, but because this is the reality of your inner soul, a truth to which it is intrinsically bound —then you are not afraid to inquire. There is no apprehension of being proven wrong, only certitude that you shall understand more.

Therefore, only true faith can be truly objective.

320.

The intellect is the ultimate frontier of G-dliness, for
the Zohar says, "No thought can grasp Him at all."
Ultimately, G-dliness must come to dwell even in that
place which by definition cannot contain Him. The
mind must struggle to understand all that it can, and
then even harder to know that which it cannot know.

321.

Many people, without realizing, end up with two gods:

One god is an impersonal one, an all-encompassing,
transcendent force.

But then, at times of trouble, they cry out to another,
personal god, with whom they have an intimate
relationship.

Our faith is all about knowing that these two are one.
The same G-d who is beyond all things, He is the same
one who hears your cries and counts your tears. The
same G-d who is the force behind all existence and
transcends even that, He is the same G-d who cares
about what is cooking in your kitchen and how you
treat your fellow man.

G-d cannot be defined, even as transcendent. He is
beyond all things and within them at once.

322.

Faith is not the result of past experience. On the contrary, faith is an act that comes from within and *creates* experience. Things happen because you trust they will.

323.

Belief is not enough—you need Trust. A believer can be a thief and a murderer. Trust in G-d changes the way you live.

324.

Do you know why American money is so successful? Because it has written on it, "In G-d We Trust". Not just *"Believe". "Trust"*.

Furthermore, the money even tells you its purpose: Upon it is written, "E Pluribus Unum". The purpose of all your dealings with money is to make from many a Oneness. And if that is truly your purpose, then you will rely on the One Creator to provide your needs.

325.

Judaism works. We have 3300 years of testing under every possible condition to prove that. How and why it works is not really so relevant. Is there anyone who refuses to eat because he has not yet fathomed the workings of the digestive tract?

326.

In life, we almost never wait for 100% guarantees. We trust that the dentist is a dentist, the taxi driver is a taxi driver, and so on—and put our lives in their hands—on flimsy tacit evidence. Yet, when it comes to a simple good deed, people demand 100% proof that this is really what G-d wants them to do!

SCIENCE AND TECHNOLOGY

The Rebbe studied both sciences and the humanities at the University of Berlin and at the Sorbonne.

Throughout the nineteenth century and for most of the twentieth, rabbis dealt with the "challenge of science". Generally, their approach was the classic one of apologetics, redefining tradition so it would not conflict with what science seemed to say.

The Rebbe was intolerant of such apologetics as though it were ipecac. To him there was no conflict to begin with, only a gross misunderstanding of what science is and what it says.

327.

Einstein received acclaim for demonstrating that energy and matter are one. The scientist who demonstrates how *all* forces are one in a unified theory will receive even greater acclaim. So, since we all agree that someone will eventually establish this, why not accept it right now, and we'll call it G-d?

328.

Everything was created as a means to know G-d. Every discovery we have ever made was planted here in the six days of creation in order that we utilize it for a G-dly purpose.

329.

Over 1700 years in advance, the author of the Zohar predicted a revolution of science that would take place about the date 1840. There he describes the fountains of wisdom bursting forth from the ground and flooding the earth—all in preparation for an era when the world shall be filled with wisdom and knowledge of the Oneness of its Creator.

From this we know that the true purpose of all technology and modern science is neither convenience nor power, but a means to discover G-dliness within the physical world.

330.

Every revelation of modern science can be found hidden in the Torah. Even quantum mechanics—if you understand Torah well enough.

331.

Science presents no challenge to Torah. Scientists, perhaps, but not Science.

True Science can only enhance Torah by demonstrating its truths in the empirical realm.

Communication technologies have provided us a metaphor to comprehend how One Being can perceive all things in a single instance. It makes you wonder how previous generation could possibly have understood such things.

Modern physics has brought us to a realization of the oneness of our universe, from which we may better grasp the Oneness of its Creator: All that exists can be divided into two elements: The force, and the particle that bears that force. In other terms: quality and quantity. With a simple equation, Einstein demonstrated that even these two elements are truly one.

332.

The scientist's understanding begins from the outside and attempts to work in—from the bottom up. He begins with subjective empiricism in an attempts to deduce an objective model.

The wisdom of he who knows Torah begins from the inside and works its way out—from the top down. He meditates upon the Creator's own objective model and applies it to discover the truth behind this world.

333.

No one has ever seen, touched or measured a particle or a wave of gravity. Furthermore, the very notion of gravity is mystifying: Masses light years apart with nothing between them, affecting each other's movements!

Yet we all accept there must be a cause behind the phenomena we observe, so we call this elusive force "gravity".

So too, there is a cause behind existence. That Cause may be even more elusive, but the reality of its existence is at least as inescapable and empirically evident.

BONDING WITH
A TZADDIK

This is something the American cowboy finds real hard—but the truth is, every seeker needs a guide and nobody pulls himself up by tugging at his own hair.

But a rebbe is much more. A rebbe is a guide who becomes one with you. Your search becomes his search, your struggle, his struggle. You look into the words of your rebbe and you find yourself there.

Just as the soul of Adam contained all souls that were to come from him, so the soul of a rebbe, says chassidic tradition, contains the soul of every one of his chassidim.

334.

When Abraham went down to Egypt, he asked of his wife, Sarah, "Please say you are my sister."

The bond between a man and a woman in marriage is a powerful one, but still not as essential as that of brother and sister. A marriage is two parts that bond as one in a fire of passion—but still two parts that may, therefore, be somehow torn apart. When the passion dies, the marriage is weakened. The passion is renewed, and the marriage is healed.

But a brother and sister began as one, and remain one inseparably—whether there is passion or not, or even the opposite.

Abraham, as he descended from the Holy Land into the darkness of Egypt, knew that his only hope of surviving immersion in such impurity would be to bond as intimately as possible with an enlightened, wholly transcendent soul that would remain beyond all this.

And so, he asked Sarah to say she was his sister.

...

The previous rebbe, Rabbi Yosef Yitzchaak
Schneerson, left behind a vast and invaluable library.
Several of his inheritors claimed the books were
private property of Rabbi Yosef Yitzchaak, and
therefore belonged to them. The Rebbe claimed they
were collected for the chassidim and therefore still
belonged to the chassidim. After over 35 years of
contention, the issue finally ended up in court.

When the lawyers put the question of ownership to the
previous rebbe's daughter, the wife of the Rebbe, she
replied,

"My father and his library belong to the chassidim."

The Rebbe later repeated her words publicly and
declared that these were the words that won the case.

335.

When the Rebbe accepted the leadership of Lubavitch,
after a year of constant pressure and pleading from
the chassidim, he announced:

Don't think you're going to hold on to my prayer shawl
for a free ride. I will provide whatever I can. But each
one must do his own job himself.

336.

The tzaddik connects you with your G-d—and then
gets out of the way.

337.

A college student asked the Rebbe what is his job. "A rabbi's job," he said, "I understand. He lectures everybody to make them feel guilty. But what is a rebbe?"

The Rebbe gestured to the ceiling of his room and replied:

Do you see that light bulb? It is connected by wires to a power plant that powers the whole of Brooklyn. And that plant is connected to turbo-generators at Niagara Falls that power the whole of New York State and more.

Every one of us is a light bulb wired in to a powerful generator. But the room is still dark. The job of a rebbe is to take your hand in the dark room and place it on the switch that makes the connection to that generator.

338.

Speaking about his relationship with his rebbe:

This is the feeling of a chassid: Just as the Zohar says that we, the Torah and our G-d are all one, so too, the chassid, his rebbe and his G-d are all one. I haven't seen this written anywhere, so you can argue all you want. But this is how I feel and I know it is true.

339.

Sometimes a thought of the Rebbe comes, hitting at the gut level, carrying with it a yearning, a thirst, a quiet fire of the sort that tears you apart from the inside.

Was it because I was thinking of the Rebbe?

Or because the Rebbe was thinking of me?

A rebbe knows his chassidim as one knows his own eyes and ears and fingers and toes. A chassid feels his rebbe as one feels the beating of his own heart.

340.

The rebbes of Lubavitch had a time put aside to think about their chassidim, each one individually, with all the love and fondness they had for them.

As water reflects the face that looks into it, so the heart of man responds to the thoughts another thinks of him. And this way the chassidim and their rebbe are bound together in an eternal bond of love.

341.

The Tzaddik lacks nothing and so he prays for his people.

But if he lacks nothing, then he knows that in truth they also lack nothing, and if so, for what is he praying?

He prays they should have open eyes and open hearts to see and to know that in truth they lack nothing.

But how can one who lacks nothing pray?

Because deep inside he lacks nothing, but deeper, at his very core, he is his people.

342.

When you see the darkness of the exile thickening and the trials are reaching an extreme, the only way to break the darkness is to strengthen your connection with the tzaddik of your generation.

343.

When you are doing his work, the tzaddik gives you strength. Much more strength than you could imagine.

In truth, you become one with him. His decisions become your decisions and your decisions become his decisions. There can be no greater unity of two individuals.

344.

To one who's self is his body, death of the body is death of the self. But for a tzaddik, whose self is his love, awe and faith, there is no death, only a passing. From a state of confinement to the body he makes the passage to liberation. He continues to work within this world, and even more so than before.

The Talmud says that Jacob, our father, never died. Moses, also, never died. Neither did Rabbi Judah, the Prince. They were very high souls who were one with Truth in an ultimate bond—and since Truth can never die, neither could they.

Yes, in our eyes we see death. A body is buried in the ground and we must mourn the loss. But this is only part of the falseness of our world. In the World of Truth they are still here as before.

And the proof: We are still here. For if these high souls would not be with us in our world, all that we know would cease to exist.

345.

A Tzaddik never leaves this world—he transcends it, but he is still within it. He is still there to assist those who are bond to him with blessing and advice, just as before, and even more so. Even those who did not know him in his corporeal lifetime can still create with him an essential bond.

The only difference is in us: Now we must work harder to connect.

...

Throughout the Rebbe's leadership, he persistently answered people's requests for blessings, "I will bring this to the attention of my father-in-law at his grave site."

Whenever the Rebbe used the words, "The Rebbe", he meant his late father-in-law, the previous rebbe. In the Rebbe's world, his rebbe never died.

DAYS ARE COMING...

It is an ancient tradition that in every generation there is one tzaddik above all others who is the heart of all those alive on the face of the earth. When one passes on, another takes over.

The tzaddik is the transparent channel through which all life flows on its way to the Creation and all its beings. He or she is the seat of the megaconsciousness of all minds and all souls. The tzaddik is us and we are the tzaddik and in the tzaddik we are one.

This is my gut feeling: The Rebbe was the heart of the Boomers and of all those born in their wake.

Then, sometimes, I look at the face of the Rebbe, and I think, "This, my heart? But we are so distant! His world, my world...I am he and he is me?! If he is my own heart, then how do I feel such a stranger to him?!"

But then, do you feel your heart beating within you? Most people will answer they don't and cannot, unless they search for a pulse somewhere. But isn't that absurd: Your entire body is incessantly throbbing in every limb and organ with the relentless pumping of the heart—and you say you do not feel it? It is just that it is so close to you, so much you, that you cannot feel it, just as you do not notice your own nose in front of you.

All events of body and mind reflect the nuances of the beating of the heart and of the life-giving blood that passes through it.

All our searching for higher fulfillment, all our rejection of the established order, all our awaiting of "the Aquarian Age" or "the New Age" or whatever you want to call it—all is an expression of the flow of life that comes to us through the tzaddik. The tzaddik, however, meant the same Messianic Era that all our great-grandparents had been waiting for.

And still does, because he is still here with us.

346.

1951: We are the last generation of the exile and the first of a new age.

1967: A mighty wind of return is blowing. I hear the sound of a great ram's horn. The souls of the young people are preparing for Moshiach.

1990: The time line of Mankind, according to tradition, is divided into six millennium corresponding to the six days of Creation. The seventh millennium is beyond time.

According to this paradigm, the year 5751 (October 1990–September 1991) equates with high noon on the sixth day.

The year 5751 begins an entirely new era. Just as on Friday afternoon we begin the mad rush to prepare for the seventh day, so too all the wonders you will see in this year are nature's frenzy to prepare for a time beyond time. We are about to enter what the ancient sages referred to as the Era of Moshiach.

347.

Over 1800 years ago, the author of the Zohar predicted a revolution of science that would take place about the date 1840. There he describes the floodgates of heaven above and the fountains of wisdom below bursting forth from the ground and flooding the earth—all in preparation for an era when the world shall be filled with wisdom and knowledge of the Oneness of its Creator.

The wisdom from above are the innermost secrets of the Torah that have been revealed to the chassidic masters.

The wisdom from below is the new understanding of the oneness of the creation that has been revealed by modern science.

And now all is prepared.

348.

"And the world shall be filled with the awareness of G-d as the waters cover the ocean floor."—Isaiah

These are the Waters of Life To All Things.

Now we live as creatures of the dry land, as though we were separate beings from our life source. Then we shall be as creatures of the sea that live absorbed within their source of life. We shall be in such oneness with the Source of All Life until there shall be nothing to distinguish between the created being and the Creator.

349.

There were others in the past who shouted "Moshiach is coming! Sell your homes and leave to the Holy Land!"

The Rebbe shouted, "Moshiach is on his way! Build homes! Build institutions! Do everything you can now, so we can shlep it all with us!"

There are some who are afraid of a new age. They wonder, "What will happen to my career? My whole lifestyle will have to change! What about all the acquaintances and connections I've spent a lifetime building? And what about all my worldly possessions, my retirement plan, my investments? Will they take my car away?"

Even these people have nothing to fear. The Age of Moshiach is not something separate from our times. It is pieced together from everything we do now, and all that we know of shall remain. Only the negativity will vanish, and the G-dliness within each thing will be obvious for us to see.

350.

The material world is a place where each thing seems to say, "Here I am and here I always was."— as though it has no source.

In fact, only the Essence of All Things has no source. He was and is and always will be. This is the truth of what our world is trying to tell us: It is only trying to express—in a distorted way—its own true essence, the Essence of All Things that has no source. In the times of Moshiach the distortion shall vanish and we shall see clearly nothing but that Essence.

351.

Everything has its limits, even darkness. As the Zohar
says, "When the world was made, a limit was set how
long it will function in confusion."

352.

We are not waiting for some great revelation from
above to save us from our incompetence as guardians
of this world and put everything in order. Rather, we
are waiting to see the sun rise over everything we have
done, to see the fruits of our labors blossom in an
eternal spring.

...

A New Age comes upon the world as a spring rain
upon a plowed and seeded field. Plow and sow now,
while there is still time.

353.

It will happen with you or without you, whether you
believe in it or not. True, you could help it be sooner.
But the fact is, it will be in our times whether you help
or not. And it will be good for you, no matter what.

But have you asked yourself, "Where will I be standing
when that time comes? What will I be involved in? Will I
be part of it, or will it be despite me?"

354.

People ask, "But how could you see so much good in
the future when so much evil predominates now
—and it grows day by day?"

But such is the order of things: Darkness was only
placed in the world to challenge light. As the light
intensifies, the darkness thickens to defy it.

355.

They say the most profound darkness comes just
before the dawn. The harshest oppression of our
forefathers in Egypt came just before their liberation.

That was a coarse darkness of slavery of the body.
Today it is a darkness of the soul, a deep slumber of
the spirit of Man. There are sparks of light,
glimmerings of a sun that never shone before—but
the darkness of night overwhelms all.

Prepare for dawn.

356.

A parable:

A father answers the questions of his child and they are happy together, in joyful dialogue.

Then the child asks a question, and the father must think deeply—not just for the answer, but to reach to the essence of this answer so he may bring it to the world of his child. For a long while, the father is quiet.

And so, the child becomes anxious and begins to cry. "Father, where are you? Why do you no longer talk to me? Why have you deserted me for your own thoughts?"

And then the father begins to speak, but this time it is the deepest core of his mind that flows into the mind and heart of the child. Such a flow that with this the child, too, may become a father.

The child is us. The time of silence is now.

When the spirit of Man is dark, when the flow gates of Above seem all but sealed, prepare for liberation.

357.

If you believe the universe has a Creator, then you surely recognize that the creation must have a purpose.

Now, take a look around you. This is definitely not the purpose.

The purpose is in a time yet to come. This is just a way of getting there.

358.

You build a dream house.

You start with a dream. The dream becomes a plan. The plan becomes a lot of dirty work. The dirty work becomes a house.

If you are successful, it is the house of your dreams.

Dream, plan, dirty work, success. Why is this the fundamental strategy of all human endeavor? Because it is the story of the universe.

Those who can feel the dream, those who can read the plan, they see we are now at the finishing touches.

359.

Before I had even started school, a picture of liberation was already forming in my mind. Such a liberation, and in such a way, that it shall truly make sense of all the suffering, all the oppression and persecution we have undergone.

It is not that there will be no more darkness, no more suffering, that those things shall cease to exist. It will be such an essence-light that darkness itself will become light— *even the darkness and suffering of the past.*

360.

On the awesome day of Rosh Hashana, the Jewish New Year, of the year 5507 (1746), the Baal Shem Tov lay in deep meditation and ascended to the holy chamber of the Moshiach.

"Master," he asked, "when shall you come?"

The answer: "When your wellsprings shall spread to the outside."

The wellspring are the wellsprings of the deepest inner wisdom.

Not only the *water* of the wellsprings, but the *wellsprings* themselves must spread forth. When the furthest, darkest reaches of the material world shall become wellsprings of the innermost wisdom, then the Moshiach shall come.

This is our mandate now.

361.

The present state of the world is called *gola* (גולה). The state of the world as it will soon be is called *geula* (גאולה).

The two words are exactly the same, except that "geula" has the letter *alef* (א) inserted in the middle.

"Alef" means "master". It also means "one".

To make *gola* into *geula*, we only need reveal the alef—the One Master of the Universe who is hidden within the artifacts of our present world.

362.

It is not so much that we need to be taken out of exile.
It is that the exile must be taken out of us.

363.

Late Spring, 1991: Live now with the New Age. Study
about it. Talk about it. Look intently into every detail of
our world now and imagine how it will be in those
times. Be there now. Not just to hasten its coming, but
to be prepared to receive its good.

364.

Autumn 1991, a few months before his fatal stroke:
After 3307 years, all that's needed has been done. The
table is set, the feast of Moshiach is being served with
the Ancient Wine, the Leviathan and the Wild Ox—and
we are sitting at it.

All that's left is to open our eyes and see.

*Those last words I write, but I do not understand.
But then, if I understood them, I suppose I would
not need to be told to open my eyes.*

Days Are Coming

TRANSMISSION

365.

After the Rebbe's wife, Rebbetzin Chaya Mushka, daughter of the previous rebbe of Lubavitch, Rabbi Yosef Yitzchaak Schneerson, passed on, the Rebbe began to spend more and more time at the "ohel"—the burial site of the previous Rebbe. The Rebbe would stand there for many hours, with an almost empty stomach, reading people's letters to him and saying psalms.

On the 28th of Nisan, 5751 (1991), the Rebbe returned from the ohel, said the evening prayers, and began to speak to the crowd. In the midst of his talk, unexpectedly, came the following words:

"...As we are talking about the geula so much at this time, a disturbing question arises: How is it possible that, despite everything, we have not yet achieved the advent of Moshiach? This is entirely beyond comprehension!

And another distressing issue: Many Jews are gathered together, and at such an opportune time for the geula—and nevertheless they do not storm the gates and demand Moshiach immediately! It is not inconceivable to them that, G-d forbid, Moshiach may not come tonight...or tomorrow...or the next day—G-d forbid!

Even when they do cry out, singing and shouting, "How much longer?!", they do this only because they have been told to do so. But if they would mean it and cry out truthfully, there is no doubt Moshiach would already have come!

What more can I do so that all the Jewish People should cry out sincerely and thereby make Moshiach real? After all that I have done, nothing has helped. And the proof: We are still in exile. And most important, in an inner spiritual exile.

The only thing I am able to do is hand the matter over to you. Do everything you can—in a way of the "Lights of Tohu", but into the "Vessels of Tikun"* —to bring Moshiach into our reality immediately.

May it be His will that, eventually, there will be ten Jews that will stubbornly resolve to wrestle and demand of G-d—and certainly they shall succeed —to bring the immediate redemption, as it is written,

---

[1] *Tohu and Tikun are spiritual worlds discussed in Jewish mysticism. Tohu has great light and energy, but is unable to contain it. Tikun has orderly, harmonious vessels to contain the light, but the light is not as great.*

"...for they are a stiff necked people and so You shall pardon our sins and our wrongdoings and make us Your possession."

So I have done my part. From this point on, do whatever *you* can.

And may it be His will that there will be one of you, or two, or three, that will come up with a suggestion of what to do and how to do it. And especially—and this is the main thing—that you should actually accomplish it and bring the true and complete geula immediately, right now, and out of joy and a good heart.

After the Rebbe spoke these words, a great spirit of inspiration swept through Lubavitch. For the next eleven months the Rebbe spoke every week on the topic of Moshiach and encouraged every person to study whatever he or she could about the geula, and to do whatever could be done to publicize the matter.

After eleven months, the Rebbe cleared his desk, went to the ohel, and fell there from a major stroke. Although unable to speak more than a few words, he continued providing guidance and counsel from his bed and armchair. Two years later to that very same day, the Rebbe suffered another stroke. Three months and a few days afterwards, the Rebbe passed on.

...

The Rebbe believed in our orphaned, post-holocaust generation. We won't let him down.

"So I have done my part. From this point on,
do whatever *you* can."

APPENDICES

- The Seven Instructions of Noah
- My People
- Glossary

Appendices

THE SEVEN INSTRUCTIONS OF NOAH

At the dawn of creation G-d gave the first human being six rules to follow in order that His world be sustained. Later, after the Great Flood, he charged Noah with one more. So it is recounted in the Book of Genesis as interpreted by our tradition in the Talmud.

For most of Jewish history, circumstance did not permit our people to promulgate these principles, other than by indirect means. When the Rebbe began speaking about publicizing them as a preparation for a new era, he was reviving an almost lost tradition.

What fascinates me is the breathing room they provide. They are like the guidelines of a great master of music or art: firm, reliable and comprehensive—but only a base, and upon this base each people and every person may build.

According to the sages of the Talmud, there are 70 families with 70 paths within the great Family of Man. And each individual has his or her path within a path. Yet there is one universal basis for us all.

Anyone who lives by these rules, acknowledging that they are what G-d wants of us, is considered by our tradition to be righteous. That person is a builder with a share in the world as it is meant to be.

Here are those seven instructions, according to ancient tradition, with a touch of elaboration:

1. Acknowledge that there is only one G-d who is Infinite and Supreme above all things. Do not replace that Supreme Being with finite idols, be it yourself, or other beings. In this command is included such acts as prayer, study and meditation.

2. Respect the Creator. As frustrated and angry as you may be, do not vent it by cursing your Maker.

3. Do not murder. Each human being, just as Adam and Eve, comprises an entire world. To save a life is to save that entire world. To destroy a life is to destroy an entire world. To help others live is a corollary of this principle.

4. Respect the institution of marriage. Marriage is a most divine act. The marriage of a man and a woman is a reflection of the Oneness of G-d and His creation. Dishonesty in marriage is an assault on that Oneness.

5. Do not steal. Deal honestly in all your business. By relying on G-d rather than on our own conniving, we express our trust in Him as the Provider of Life.

6. Respect G-d's creatures. At the outset of his creation, Man was the gardener in the Garden of Eden to "take care of it and protect it". At first, Man was forbidden to harm any animal. After the Great Flood, he was permitted to consume meat—but with a warning: Do not cause unnecessary suffering to any creature.

7. Maintain justice. Justice is G-d's business, but we are given the charge to lay down necessary laws and enforce them whenever we can. When we right the wrongs of society, we are acting as partners in the act of sustaining the creation.

MY PEOPLE

People want to know how the Rebbe attracted so many admirers. It's really quite a simple formula:

Many became leaders because they brought their people to believe in them. The Rebbe was a great leader because he believed so much in his people.

...

If you find a Jew who has love of G-d, but lacks love of his people and love of Torah, tell him that this love cannot last.

If you find a Jew who has love of his people, but lacks love of G-d and love of Torah, work with him to nurture this love until it overflows into the other two, until all three join in one tight knot that will never be untied.

...

Hormones, vitamins, chromosomes, etc., make up only a minuscule portion of the body—yet they are the most crucial elements of life.

Jews are the smallest minority of all the peoples of the world—yet they are the most vital element of history.

...

The Jewish People are the heart of the world. If they are healthy, the world is healthy.

...

To a rabbi who wrote about "secular Jews":

You categorize them as religious Jews and secular Jews! How dare you make such a distinction! There is no such thing as a secular Jew. All Jews are holy.

...

The Torah speaks about four sons. One wise, one wicked, one in a state of wonder, one who does not realize he should ask. What do they all have in common? "One". As in, "Listen Israel, G-d our Lord, G-d is One!"

That "One" is the essence of every Jew—even the one the Torah calls "wicked".

...

There are no heretics nowadays. You have to know an awful lot to be a heretic.

...

At the onset of the Persian Gulf crisis, a certain prominent rabbi in Israel was preaching that the Jews were about to be punished for the sinners amongst them. They told me they had never seen the Rebbe angry before::

The sages tell us that our father Jacob never died. "Since his children are alive, he is alive."

Each and every Jew is the personification of his father Jacob, and the heart of each and every Jew is alive and beating strong. To say about any one of them that he is spiritually dead is to pronounce our father Jacob dead. If to you it appears that way, the fault is in you, not in the Jew you observe.

G-d sees only good in them. He will make great miracles for them and they will be safe.

...

The Jewish people are one. A Jew putting on tefillin in America affects the safety of a Jewish soldier in Israel.

...

Every Jew has a mitzvah to which he finds an affinity. Don't argue with him. Find that mitzvah and encourage him in it.

...

It is our nature that each one of us finds it impossible to knowingly separate himself from our G-d.

...

After many years, some began to follow the Rebbe's lead and reach out to Jews who were not living a traditional Jewish life. They called it, "Bringing close those who are distant". The term did not find favor in the Rebbe's eyes. He wrote:

You say you are "bringing close those who are distant"?! What gives you the right to call them distant and pretend you are close? You must approach each one as though you were an emissary sent by the King of kings of kings to talk with the prince, his only son!

GLOSSARY

Alter Rebbe .... Rabbi Schneur Zalman of Liadi, 1745–1812. Author of the Tanya and Shulchan Aruch HaRav. First in the line of the Rebbes of Lubavitch.

Akiva .... Rabbi Akiva was a great scholar and social activist, the most outstanding Jewish figure of the Roman Era.

Baal Shem Tov .... Rabbi Yisroel ben Eliezer, 1698–1760. Father of the chassidic movement.

Chanuka .... An eight day celebration of the Maccabean victory over the ancient Syrian-Greek oppressors. Each day, another candle is added to the candelabra ("menorah") until eight are lit on the final day.

Chassid .... Generally, one who goes beyond the letter of the law. In the sense it is used herein, one who lives the teachings of a chassidic master.

Chassidim .... Plural of chassid.

G-d......................In Jewish belief, any word that is used as an appellation of G-d must be treated respectfully. It is common to avoid spelling out the entire word in case the paper upon which it is written be discarded in an undignified manner.

Geula......................Liberation or redemption from exile and oppression. Generally used to describe the transitory stage into the Messianic Era.

Kaballa....................Literally, "tradition". Generally refers to the mystic tradition which is an integral part of Judaism.

Lubavitch................See page 13.

Midrash..................An ancient elaboration of the stories of the Bible.

Mitzvah...................Literally, "commandment". Also carries the meaning of "connection". Any act prescribed by the Torah. Often used in the sense of "a good deed".

Moshiach................Literally, "the Anointed". The leader of the Jewish people who will reign at the end of the exile and bring us all into a new era of peace and spiritual enlightenment.

Rebbe....................Literally, "My Teacher". Term used to denote a chassidic master.

Shabbos................The Sabbath. But it sounds so much more delicious in Yiddish.

Tammuz................The name of the 4th month of the Jewish calendar.

Tefillin..................The black leather boxes that are placed on the arm and head at the time of prayer. Inside are small parchment scrolls.

Torah....................Literally, "teaching". Most specifically, the five books of Moses. Less specifically, all the works of the prophets and the oral tradition. In its most general sense, all the teachings of Jewish sages throughout the ages that grew out of the written and oral tradition, such as the Talmud, Zohar, the classic commentaries, and so on.

Tzaddik.................Literally, a righteous person. In Chassidic thought, one who has conquered his animal soul.

Tzemach Tzedek ....Rabbi Menachem Mendel of Lubavitch, the 3rd rebbe in the line of rebbes of Lubavitch. The Rebbe carries his name.

Yeshiva.................A place of Torah learning.

NOTES

NOTES

Acknowledgments

Jonathan Petrie jump-started this project.

The writing and publication of this book was made possible through the self-sacrifice, enormous patience and understanding, as well as editorial assistance, of my treasured wife.

Abouts

Rabbi Menachem Mendel Schneerson, known worldwide as "The Lubavitcher Rebbe", or just "the Rebbe", is considered by many the greatest Jewish sage of the post-war era. Seventh in a prestigious line of chassidic masters, he remarkably managed to bridge and fuse authentic old-world mysticism with the spirit of the New World.

From the time the Rebbe came to America in 1941, people of all faiths and all walks of life travelled from afar to seek his advice and hear his wisdom. Politicians, civil rights activists, writers, scientists, religious leaders, scholars, business people, and the common man and woman lined up at his door for many hours every week. Sacks of mail arrived daily, with requests for guidance and blessings from every corner of the world. His students compiled over forty volumes of his talks, which he edited.

In 1983, on the occasion of the his 80th birthday, the U.S. Congress proclaimed Rabbi Schneerson's birthday, "Education Day, USA" and awarded the Rebbe the National Scroll of Honor.

In 1995, the Rebbe was posthumously awarded the Congressional Gold Medal, an award granted only 130 Americans since Thomas Jefferson, for "outstanding and lasting contributions".

In the words of Nobel Peace Prize Laureate, Elie Wiesel, "Whenever I would see the Rebbe, he touched the depth in me. That is true of every person who came to see the Rebbe. Somehow, when the person left, he or she felt that they had lived deeper and higher, on a higher level, on a deeper sense of life and a quest for life and for meaning."

This book offers a taste of his teachings, culled from over 50 years of letters, public talks, private conversations and written works, presented in an accessible format.

Tzvi Freeman was born in Vancouver, Canada, where he became involved at an early age in Yoga, Tao and radical politics. In 1975, he left a career as an accomplished classical guitarist and composer to learn the ways of the Talmud and Jewish mysticism for nine years in the Rebbe's yeshivas. While there, he was one of the forming members of the Baal Shem Tov Band, an original synthesis of chassidic soul and song with American hard rock.

Since receiving his rabbinical ordination and completing post-graduate studies at the Rabbinical College of Canada, Tzvi has resided in Vancouver with his wife, Naomi Polichenco, and their children.

Rabbi Freeman is well known to net-surfers for his controversial essays on Judaism and the New Spirituality, as well as for his leading-edge articles on Multimedia Design. He is also an award winning designer of children's software and a popular storyteller.

Rabbi Freeman presently lectures at the University of British Columbia on Multimedia Design and Human Interface.